THE UNSTOPPABLE HOPEFULNESS

A Prophetic Journey of Faith, Resilience, and Hope

Volume 1

Prophetess
Marie Scott Wilson, PhD
(Amb.)

@2025 Copyright

All rights reserved. MARIE Global Publishing LLC

A Legacy of Grace & Divine Excellence.

United States of America

No part of this book may be reproduced, distributed, or transmitted in any form or by any means, electronic or mechanical, including photocopying, recording, or any information storage and retrieval system, without prior written permission from the publisher, except as permitted by law.

ISBN: 979-0994320-1-9

TABLE OF CONTENTS

ACKNOWLEDGMENTS V

DEDICATION VIII

PREFACE X

INTRODUCTION 1

SPECIAL SECTION OF DIVINE GRACE (VOLUME 1) 5

   Divine Protection, Authority & God's Appointed Time 5

      Volume I Foundational Truths 9

      Author Declaration, Volume I............................ 9

THE CHAPTER 1 – THE LIVING ROCK ... 10

   Standing Firm When Everything Shakes 10

CHAPTER 2 – WHEN FAITH MEETS FEAR 26

   Trusting God in the Shadows of Uncertainty 26

      CHAPTER 3 – THE POWER OF STILL BELIEVING 36

   The Power of Still Believing: When Hope Refuses to Die 36

CHAPTER 4 – WHEN PURPOSE FEELS PAINFUL 49

   The Breaking that Builds You 49

      When Pain Feels Like Rejection 50

Outgrowing What Used to Fit 51
The Sacredness of the Breaking 52
Stillness in the Middle of the Pain 53
Faith Reflection 54
Reflection Guide and Grace Journal 55

CHAPTER 5 – GRACE IN THE WAITING ROOM 57

When God Seems Silent but Heaven Is Working 57
Faith Reflection 62
Affirmations.. 63
Grace Journal 65

CHAPTER 6 – BE STILL AND KNOW 66

When Movement Stops but Miracles Begin 66
  Stillness Is Not Doing Nothing................................ 67
  When Striving Becomes a Substitute for Trust 69
  Stillness Makes Room for Divine Alignment 71
  The Strength of Holy Silence 72
  Faith Reflection 74
Reflection Guide and Grace Journal 75

CHAPTER 7 – WHEN FAITH FEELS FRAGILE 77

Holding On When You Can Barely Believe 77

Reflection Guide and Grace Journal 83

Chapter 8 – THE OIL OF ENDURANCE 84

Grace to Keep Going When Strength Runs Out 84

Reflection Guide and Grace Journal 90

CHAPTER 9 – The Courage to Begin Again 92

When Grace Gives You a Second Sunrise 92

Reflection Guide and Grace Journal 99

CHAPTER 10 – THE UNSTOPPABLE HOPE 101

The Light That Refuses to Die Out 101

    Hope That Breathes in the Dark 102

    Hope Is Not Denial. Hope Is Defiance. 103

    The Light That Refuses to Die Out 104

    Faith Reflection 104

Reflection Guide & Grace Journal 107

Reflection Guide and Grace Journal 107

CONCLUSION 109

When the Storm Doesn't Get the Last Word 109

About the Author 115

References 117

ACKNOWLEDGMENTS

With a grateful heart and a reverent spirit, I pause to acknowledge the people and the places God has used to strengthen me through every season that led to these pages. A book may carry one name on its cover, but it is never carried by one life alone. Behind every chapter are prayers that lifted me, hands that helped me, voices that encouraged me, and quiet acts of love that kept me standing when the road felt long. If these words have reached your hands, know that they were born in the presence of God and supported by the faithfulness of many.

To my family, I offer my deepest thanks. You have been more than relatives to me. You have been a shelter, a steady place, a living reminder of God's kindness. Thank you for the ways you stood with me when you did not have all the details, for the ways you believed in me when I was still learning how to believe in myself, and for the ways you carried joy and burden together with grace. Your love has been a quiet strength behind my assignment, and your prayers have covered me in moments when words could not.

To my spiritual children, I thank God for the sacred bond we share. You have been one of the great blessings of my life, and the evidence that ministry is not an idea, but a living relationship. Thank you for trusting me, for growing with me, and for allowing God to shape us together. You have reminded me that obedience bears fruit, that faith multiplies, and that God's work in us is always bigger than what we see at the start. Your lives are part of this testimony, and I honor the grace of God upon you.

To my brothers and sisters in Christ, thank you for your prayers, your encouragement, and your faith in the call upon my life. Thank you for standing with me in seasons of both clarity and uncertainty, for speaking life when weariness tried to settle in, and for walking beside me with compassion. The family of faith is one of God's great gifts, and I do not take it lightly. You have reminded me, again and again, that the Lord sustains His servants through community, counsel, and consistent intercession.

To every reader who found courage through these words, I bless you. If you turned these pages while carrying grief, uncertainty, disappointment, or fatigue, I want you to know that you are not alone. God sees you. God knows your name. God understands the private battles others never notice. My prayer is that this book becomes a lamp for your path, a gentle companion in your waiting, and a reminder that hope is not a fragile wish but a strong spiritual anchor. May you find fresh strength to rise again. May you hear God's voice even in quiet seasons. May you discover that the same Lord who carried me will also carry you.

To my beloved homeland, Liberia, I speak with love and reverence. You are more than soil and sky to me. You are not merely a place on a map. You are a people, a story, a burden, and a blessing resting deep within my spirit. You are the heartbeat of a divine assignment entrusted to me by God

Almighty. I carry you in prayer, I carry you in vision, and I carry you in hope. May your sons and daughters rise with wisdom, courage, unity, and love for one another. May the Lord heal what has been wounded, restore what has been broken, and awaken a generation that chooses integrity, peace, and righteousness. May Liberia shine with the beauty of God's purpose and the strength of a renewed moral foundation.

To every woman, every youth, and every dreamer, I offer this blessing. May this book ignite your will to live with grace, to walk with purpose, and to hold on to unstoppable hope. May you refuse to shrink under pressure. May you refuse to surrender your calling to fear. May you remember that God's hand is upon you, and that your life is not an accident. You were created with intention, shaped by grace, and equipped for impact. If these words stir something in you, let it be a spark of holy courage. Rise. Build. Serve. Love. Believe. And let God write something beautiful through your obedience.

Above all, to God Almighty, I give all glory. He is the Author of every page, the Sustainer of every season, and the One who makes purpose stand when everything else shakes. May this work honor Him, bless His people, and point every reader toward the faithfulness of the Lord who never fails.

DEDICATION

To every soul who has faced storms and still believes in the sunrise

Life has a way of testing the strength of our faith and the depth of our hope. The storms may rage, the winds may howl, and yet, those who hold on to the promise of a new dawn are never defeated. To you who have cried in the night but still lift your eyes toward heaven at first light — you are the living testimony of God's faithfulness. May your hope continue to rise like the morning sun, shining brighter with every trial overcome. Let your faith remain as steadfast as the Rock on which you stand, and may peace guard your heart like a gentle yet powerful whisper from God, saying, "Be still, for I am with you."

To my children and family, whose love anchors my purpose

You are the reflection of God's grace in my life. Your love sustains me through long days of ministry and uncertain seasons of waiting. Every prayer you offer, every word of encouragement, and every act of kindness remind me that purpose is not carried alone; such purpose is strengthened by the hands and hearts of those who believe alongside us. You are not only my earthly family but also my partners in destiny. Together, we stand as witnesses to God's promise that love never fails and that unity under His guidance brings power, peace, and perseverance.

And to Mama Liberia

You are more than a nation. You are the song that God wrote upon my heart before I was born. Your soil carries the tears, prayers, and triumphs of generations who refused to give up.

You are a divine assignment, entrusted to me not by chance but by covenant. I see in your people the spark of God's restoration power, ready to rise, rebuild, and renew. From your coast to your hills, from your towns to your villages, may the Spirit of the Lord breathe fresh life, healing, and purpose into every heart that calls you home. I will continue to labor, preach, and pray for your peace and prosperity, because your story is God's unfolding miracle.

Be blessed, my beloved.

With abiding love and unwavering faith,
Prophetess Marie Scott Wilson, PhD (Amb.)

PREFACE

Hope is not a wish we whisper into the dark, hoping something kind will happen. Hope is a divine strategy; heaven's steady plan placed inside fragile human hearts. It is the holy insistence that God is still God when the ground shakes, when tears blur the road ahead, and when life feels like a long night with no visible dawn. In every trial, the Lord is not merely watching us endure. He is writing a new page of our strength. He is shaping endurance into character, and character into a hope that does not collapse under pressure. What looks like an interruption to you is often God's invitation to deeper trust, and what feels like the end may be the very place He begins again.

The Unstoppable Hopefulness was born out of pain, perseverance, and prophetic healing. It did not come from a sheltered life untouched by sorrow, but from a soul that has wrestled, prayed, waited, and witnessed God's restoring hand. This book stands as a living testimony that faith can revive what fear tries to bury. Fear says, "It's over." Faith replies, "God is not finished." Fear tries to dig a grave for your calling, your joy, your peace, your future. But the Spirit of God speaks life where death has tried to make its home, and He proves again that what was wounded can be healed, what was shaken can be steadied, and what was lost can be redeemed.

This volume marks the beginning of a spiritual memoir, not written to impress, but to strengthen. It calls believers to walk with courage when courage feels costly, with compassion when compassion feels heavy, and with conviction when conviction makes you stand alone. These pages are meant to feel like a warm lamp in a dim room, guiding the reader one step at a time. Each chapter offers reflection and revelation, an honest look at the places where life breaks us open, and the sacred ways God meets us there. You will find that God does not waste tears. He gathers them. He does not ignore the cracks. He fills them. He does not shame the broken parts. He uses them as a blueprint for breakthrough.

As you read, may the Lord breathe fresh strength into your spirit. May you discover that hope is not the denial of pain, but the presence of God inside pain. May you learn to stand without pretending, to heal without hiding, and to believe again even if your voice trembles. And when you finish these pages, may you rise with a quiet confidence that the One who began a good work in you will carry it to completion. The storm may have spoken loudly, but God's promise speaks longer.

INTRODUCTION

The Breath Behind Unstoppable Hope

There are seasons when life feels like a long night—when the winds of uncertainty rise, the ground beneath familiar plans shifts, and the heart learns just how much faith is required to take the next step. The Unstoppable Hopefulness — Volume I was written for that sacred space: the in-between place where questions are real, tears are honest, and yet the soul still reaches for dawn. This manuscript speaks to readers who have faced storms and still believe that God is faithful, present, and purposeful—even when the path is not clear.

At its core, this volume is more than encouragement; it is a prophetic and pastoral companion. It does not ask the reader to pretend that pain is not painful. Instead, it reveals hope as heaven's strategy—an inner strength formed by God to carry His people through pressure without collapsing. Hope here is not wishful thinking; it is spiritual resilience. It is the quiet insistence that God remains God in shaking seasons, that His promises outlast the loudest storm, and that what feels like an ending can become the very place where He begins again.

This manuscript was born from lived experience—through wrestling, prayer, waiting, and restoration. It carries a consistent message: faith can revive what fear tries to bury. Fear often speaks in finalities, declaring, "It's over," "It's too late," or "You are forgotten." Faith answers with holy steadiness: "God is not finished." These pages remind the reader that what was wounded can be healed, what was shaken can be steadied, and what was lost can be redeemed. In the hands of God, even interruption can become invitation—an opening into deeper trust, deeper alignment, and deeper maturity.

A distinctive emphasis of Volume I is its special section on Divine Protection, Authority, and God's Appointed Time. Many believers know what it is to sense the clarity of a call while also feeling the contest of the journey. Obedience can be misunderstood. Waiting can feel heavy. Silence can stretch longer than expected. In those moments, this manuscript returns the reader to a stabilizing truth: God not only calls—He keeps. When He appoints, He covers; when He assigns, He sustains; and when He speaks, His Word stands. Divine protection does not mean the absence of warfare; it means the presence of God in the middle of it, limiting what may touch you and guiding what must shape you.

The book also clarifies the nature of spiritual authority. True authority is not arrogance, volume, or self-promotion. It is spiritual weight that comes from alignment—steady confidence formed by obedience, proven by endurance, and refined by faithfulness. This manuscript honors the believer who continues to stand without applause, to serve without recognition, and to keep loving when it is easier to withdraw. It teaches that the evidence of authority is not a title but a life—fruitful, surrendered, and resilient.

Throughout the chapters, a repeated instruction emerges as both anchor and invitation: be still. Stillness in these pages is not passivity; it is trust. It is refusing to panic while God performs what only He can do. It is learning the difference between striving and surrender, between forcing doors and following grace. When movement stops, miracles can begin—not because we become inactive, but because we make room for divine alignment. The reader is encouraged to release the illusion of control and embrace a posture of peace, believing that God fights battles beyond human reach.

Each chapter is structured to function like a lamp in a dim room—offering reflection, insight, prayer, affirmation, and space for journaling. The goal is not merely to inform but to transform: to strengthen courage, heal hidden places, and rebuild hope from the inside out. The manuscript speaks to the believer whose faith has felt fragile, reminding them that God does not shame weakness—He strengthens it. Even a trembling "Lord, help me" can become the doorway to renewed confidence. In this journey, tears are not wasted; they become seeds of testimony.

The purpose of The Unstoppable Hopefulness — Volume I is therefore clear: to guide readers into a faith that endures and a hope that refuses to die out. It affirms that opposition does not cancel calling, delay does not negate promise, and silence does not signal defeat. It calls the reader to begin again when necessary, to rise with quiet courage after disappointment, and to trust that God's timing is not a denial but a protection—preparing both the person and the promise for longevity.

As you enter this volume, may these pages meet you where you are—whether you are rebuilding, waiting, grieving, healing, or daring to dream again. May you find language for your prayers, strength for your steps, and peace for your heart. And when you finish, may you carry this truth forward: hope is not finished with you yet. The storm may have spoken loudly, but God's promise speaks longer—and the hope He has placed within you is, by His grace, unstoppable.

Special Section of Divine Grace (Volume 1)

Divine Protection, Authority & God's Appointed Time

I stand firmly upon the unchanging truth that God Almighty prevails in His appointed time. History bears witness, Scripture confirms, and lived experience repeats the same refrain: the Lord is never late, never confused, and never intimidated by resistance. He moves with purpose, not panic. He works with wisdom, not haste. And when God sets a time, that time becomes a holy boundary no human hand can cancel, no enemy voice can override, and no storm can erase.

This section is set apart in Volume I to affirm the divine order, protection, and authority that govern the lives of those who are called and anointed by God. There are seasons when the call of God feels clear, yet the path forward feels contested. There are moments when obedience is misunderstood, when silence feels heavy, and when waiting stretches longer than expected. In such times, the Spirit often brings us back to a simple, stabilizing truth: God is not only the One who calls. He is also the One who keeps. He does not invite His servants into destiny and then abandon them to danger. He does not release an assignment and forget the vessel He chose to carry it.

Let it be plainly understood. It is not a declaration of self-importance, nor a trumpet blast of personal greatness. It is, rather, a reverent recognition of God's covenant responsibility toward His servants. The Lord's calling is never casual. His anointing is never careless. When He places His hand upon a life, He also places His covering. When He appoints, He defends. When He assigns, He sustains. And when He speaks, His Word stands, regardless of opposition, delay, criticism, or misunderstanding.

Divine protection does not mean the absence of warfare. It means the presence of God in the midst of it. It means that what was sent to destroy you must answer the Lord who guards you. It means that snares set in secret cannot outrun the God who sees in secret. It means that even when you cannot explain what is happening around you, heaven is not confusing about what is happening within you. God's protection is often quiet, like an unseen shield in front of an unseen threat. Many battles are won before we ever know they were fought. Many doors are closed that we never realize were meant to trap us. Many attacks lose their strength because the Lord refuses to give them permission.

Divine authority is also part of this sacred order. When God appoints a servant, He does not only send them with a message; He sends them with heaven's backing. This authority is not arrogance. It is not loudness. It is not manipulation. It is the spiritual weight that comes from alignment, the steady confidence that comes from obedience, and the holy courage that rises when a person knows they are standing where God placed them. True authority is not self-made. It is God-given. And it is proven, not by applause, but by endurance. Not by titles, but by fruit. Not by recognition, but by faithfulness.

And then there is God's appointed time, which is often the greatest test and the greatest teacher. Many people can rejoice when doors open quickly. Fewer know how to remain tender and unwavering when the door seems shut, when progress appears slow, or when the promise feels distant. Yet delay is not denial when God is the Author. Waiting is not weakness when God is working. The Lord uses time as a tool. He prepares the place and the person together. He aligns resources, relationships, and readiness. He purifies motives, strengthens character, and deepens trust. God's timing protects us from stepping into a future we are not yet prepared to carry.

So, I write this as a pastoral affirmation for every called and anointed believer who has felt pressed, questioned, opposed, or stretched by the weight of waiting. Take heart. God's order has not been broken. His covering has not been lifted. His authority has not expired. The same God who summoned you is the God who shields you. The same God who assigned you is the God who will establish you. And the same God who promised is the God who will perform—when the appointed time arrives.

When God calls, He covers. When God appoints, He defends. And when God speaks, His Word stands. There are moments in the life of faith when the road grows quiet, when questions rise like fog, and when opposition seems louder than promise. In those seasons, the believer does not survive by personality or by public approval. We stand by Scripture. We stand by the steady character of God. And we stand by this unshakable truth: what God appoints, God defends. What God anoints, God protects. What God speaks, God performs in His appointed time.

The Word of God establishes a divine boundary around those who are called and consecrated for His purposes. Psalm 105:15 (KJV) declares, **"Saying, Touch not mine anointed, and do my prophets no harm."** This is not a sentence meant to inflate human ego. It is a holy command that reveals God's covenant responsibility. The anointing is not self-assigned. It is God ordained. Therefore, the defense of the anointed is not first a human task. It is the Lord's own concern. This Scripture teaches that God guards His purpose and does not leave His servants exposed to unrestrained harm. People may misunderstand the call, question the assignment, or resist the messenger, but they cannot override the God who placed His hand upon a life.

This truth is confirmed again in 1 Chronicles 16:22 (KJV), where the same command is repeated: **"Saying, Touch not mine anointed, and do my prophets no harm."** The repetition is not accidental. It confirms the seriousness and the permanence of God's position. The Lord reiterates His command so there will be no confusion. Prophetic voices, both men and women, operate under divine covering. Opposition may arise, but harm is restricted by God's authority. When God has set a boundary, the enemy cannot cross it without permission. When God has spoken protection, no weapon can move outside the limits of His sovereign rule.

From these truths flows a simple reality that must be carried with reverence and humility. Calling carries covering. Assignment carries protection. This does not mean there will be no battles. It means the battles are not ours to fight alone. It means the burden of ultimate defense does not rest on human strength, human strategy, or human vindication. God Himself watches over what He has initiated. He does not abandon His servants in the hour of pressure. He stands as Keeper, Defender, and Judge, and He ensures that what He ordained will not be buried by what was sent to oppose it.

Exodus 14:14 (KJV) gives the believer the posture of the heart during seasons of attack, uncertainty, or delay: **"The LORD shall fight for you, and ye shall hold your peace."** There are times when faith looks like movement, and there are times when faith looks like stillness. God does not always require action. Sometimes He requires quiet trust. Silence, when commanded by God, is not weakness. It is obedience. It is confidence that the Lord is working in places human hands cannot reach. When God fights, victory is assured. When God speaks, the battle shifts. When God rises, the enemy scatters, and the servant is preserved for the assignment.

Volume I Foundational Truths

Together, these Scriptures establish a foundational truth for this volume. God defends what He appoints. God protects whom He anoints. God prevails at His appointed time. Opposition does not cancel calling. Delay does not negate promise. Silence does not signal defeat. God remains sovereign. Even when the process is slow, heaven is not confused. Even when the season is heavy, God's hand is not lifted. Even when voices rise in accusation, the Lord's verdict stands higher than human opinions.

Author Declaration, Volume I

As a believer in Christ and as a Prophetess, I trust God Almighty to continue prevailing at His appointed time. I remain anchored in His Word, obedient to His instruction, and at peace, knowing that the Lord Himself fights battles beyond human reach. I do not rest my confidence on human validation, nor do I measure God's faithfulness by temporary conditions. I place my trust in the God who calls, covers, and completes. What God has spoken shall surely come to pass.

The Chapter 1 – The Living Rock

Standing Firm When Everything Shakes

Key Scripture:

"For who is God save the LORD?
Or who is a rock save our God?"
Psalm 18:31 (KJV)

Scripture Focus: "For who?"

The Essence, Meaning, and Purpose of "The Living Rock"

This chapter is an invitation to settle your soul on One Truth that does not crack under pressure. God is not merely strong. He is steady. He is not simply present. He is permanent. "The Living Rock" means we are not leaning on an idea, a mood, or a temporary season of relief. We are leaning on the God who remains when everything else shifts. When the world trembles, the Rock does not. When a heart breaks, the Rock does not. When doors close, people change, finances fail, and plans unravel, the Rock does not move an inch.

Psalm 18:31 begins with a question that feels like a holy interruption. "For who is God save the LORD?" In other words, who else deserves the weight of your trust? Who else can carry the full burden of your life without dropping it? Who else can hold your tomorrow when you can barely manage today? Scripture is not asking for a polite answer. It is calling you to a decision. It is asking you to name what you have been leaning on, and then to compare it with the faithfulness of the Lord. The question is meant to clear the fog. It separates what is reliable from what is fragile. It exposes false foundations and gently leads us back to the One who cannot be shaken.

The Living Rock is the God who stands firm when all else trembles. He is the anchor of our souls, the solid foundation that cannot be shaken by storms or seasons. When our hope feels buried under life's rubble, His strength becomes our unbreakable place of rest. This is not poetry for the calm days only. This is survival truth for the days when your hands are tired, your mind is loud, and your heart is trying to remember how to sing again.

Faith is not the absence of hardship, but the presence of endurance through it. The Living Rock reminds us that even when the path feels uneven, the One who built it still holds us steady. Every trial becomes a testament, not to our weakness, but to God's power working through us. And this is one of the hidden mercies of suffering. Trials do not only test our strength. They reveal God's strength. They do not only expose our limits. They introduce us to His limitless care.

We learn to rest, not because everything is perfect, but because our hope is placed upon a perfect God. The Rock does not move, even when life does. In Him, we find peace that withstands pain, strength that outlasts struggle, and hope that defies the impossible. And the question rises again, this time like a quiet thunder in the soul: "Is God besides the Lord? And who is the Rock except our God?" Psalm 18:31 (NIV). The language is different, but the message is the same. There is no substitute. There is no equal. There is no other foundation that will hold when the rain becomes heavy. God is not only powerful in the hour of crisis.

He is steady in every season. Strength is what you call when something breaks, but steadiness is what holds you before anything ever shifts. The Living Rock is not a poetic symbol we reach for when we feel small, and it is not a comforting metaphor we repeat when life gets loud. The Living Rock is the solid reality of a God who does not move when everything else does. He is not startled by your struggle, and He is not pacing heaven, waiting for the right moment to act. He is already present beneath your faith, underneath your weary prayers, carrying what human hands cannot sustain and holding what human strength cannot keep together.

Many of us believe in God's power yet still wrestle with resting in His permanence. We know He can do miracles, but we quietly fear what happens if the miracle takes time. We look for relief instead of foundation, for quick answers instead of deep anchoring. Yet Scripture does not merely invite us to feel encouraged in passing moments. It calls us to examine what we are standing on. When life presses hard, when relationships strain, when plans unravel, and when disappointment begins to speak to you in a quiet way, the question is not whether God is capable. The deeper question is whether our trust is placed in something that can bear the full weight of our lives. If our confidence is built on outcomes, applause, timing, or human reliability, then the ground will eventually shift. But if our confidence is built on God Himself, then even when the winds howl and the waters rise, we are not left floating without hope.

The Living Rock is the God who does not fluctuate with circumstance. He is not seasonal, faithful only when the days are bright and the road is smooth. He is not dependent on outcomes, as though your situation must turn in a certain direction for Him to remain good. He is not altered by fear, pressure, or delay. He does not become less God because life becomes more intense. Faith rooted in Him is not sustained by emotional certainty or external stability, but by the unchanging nature of God Himself. This is why the Rock matters. When everything shakes, the Rock remains. When your strength fades, His steadiness does not. When the world feels uncertain, His presence stays sure. And when you can no longer hold yourself up, the Living Rock holds you, not with temporary comfort, but with unmovable grace.

1. A Moment of Stillness

Before every sunrise, there is a hush, that gentle space when creation remembers who holds it together.

I once stood near the Fen River, watching the water move steadily forward while the ground beneath my feet remained firm. The current carried its own strength and urgency, pressing on with purpose, yet the land did not crumble beneath it. There was no panic in the soil, no trembling in the bank. It simply held. In that quiet, unhurried moment, the Lord spoke gently to my spirit, not with thunder but with a steady whisper that reached deeper than sound: "I am the Rock beneath your river."

That word settled into me like warm oil poured over a weary heart. It reminded me that life moves, whether we are ready or not. Seasons shift. Circumstances surge and recede like rising waters. Some days flow peacefully. Other days rush with force and uncertainty. Yet beneath it all, God remains unmoved. The river does not need to stop for the land to be stable. Movement does not equal collapse. Pressure does not mean you are forsaken. Difficulty does not announce abandonment. Sometimes it is simply the sound of life passing through, while God quietly holds you in place.

So often we pray for the river to calm, and God, in His mercy, sometimes does. But there are also times when His faithfulness is not displayed by instantly changing the current, but by sustaining what is underneath it. God's stability often works beneath circumstances rather than above them. He may not always still the waters immediately, but He ensures that nothing collapses beneath them. He does not promise a life without motion, but He promises a foundation that will not fail. When you cannot control what flows toward you, you can trust the One who supports what you stand on.

This is where faith becomes more than an idea. Faith is not a theory we discuss when life is easy. It is the steady choice to lean on God when the current is strong. It is waking up with questions and still placing your feet on His promises. It is feeling the pull of fear, the weight of uncertainty, and yet discovering that you are still standing. There are moments when the clearest revelation of God's strength is not found in dramatic miracles, but in the quiet assurance that nothing has given way beneath your feet.

If you are in a season where the waters are moving fast, do not assume you are losing ground. You may be standing on the Rock without even realizing it. The current may be loud, but the foundation is sure. God is not simply watching your river from a distance. He is beneath it, holding you steady, keeping you secure, and proving again that what He supports cannot be swept away.

Thought provoking question: When life gets loud, have you learned how to return to the hush where God speaks?

2. When Everything Shakes

Shaking is not always punishment. Often, it is simplification. There are seasons when God, in His wise and tender care, allows what is unstable to be disturbed so what is unshakable can be revealed. Shaking does not automatically mean God is angry. Sometimes it means God is near, working with precision, loosening what has quietly wrapped itself around your soul and calling it security. He permits the trembling not to terrorize you, but to free you.

In the shaking, God exposes what cannot sustain you. Relationships that have become weighted instead of supportive begin to show their true strain. Identities rooted in performance start to crack under the pressure of trying to remain impressive. Expectations built on timing rather than truth begin to disappoint you, not because God has failed, but because those expectations were never meant to carry your hope. Even self-reliance can hide behind the noble word responsibility until life grows heavy enough to reveal that you were carrying more than you were ever asked to bear. Shaking pulls the mask off false strength. It brings clarity. It makes the heart honest.

What cannot hold you must be removed, not to harm you, but to establish you. There is support we cling to because they feel familiar, but familiarity is not the same as faithfulness. Some things are comfortable, but not trustworthy. And God loves you too much to let you build a life on beams that will eventually splinter. When He allows the shaking, He is not taking pleasure in your pain. He is rescuing you from collapse. He is preventing a deeper ruin by addressing the hidden cracks now.

This is why loss is not always theft. Sometimes it is mercy. God does not strip you to shame you. He strips you to save you. He removes what is unstable so your faith can rest on what is eternal. He clears away the temporarily so your heart can take hold of the everlasting. He separates you from what cannot keep you, so you can be anchored to the One who will never let you go. When everything else is shaken loose, the Rock remains.

And here is the holy mystery. God removes what cannot hold you precisely because He intends to establish you in Himself. The shaking is not evidence of His absence. It is proof of His intentional care. It is the hand of a loving Father making room for a sturdier foundation. So, if your world feels unsettled, do not assume you are being abandoned. You may be being repositioned. You may be strengthened. You may be being brought back to the Rock, where your soul can finally rest, not on what is fragile, but on what cannot be moved.

There are times when the very ground of life feels unstable, when people change, finances fail and promises collapse. It is then that we discover the difference between a foundation built on sand and one built on Spirit.

During a season of personal loss, I cried out, "Lord, why is everything falling apart?" He answered gently, "Because I am removing what cannot hold you, so that only I remain."

Every shaking reveals what is eternal. The Living Rock does not simply support us. He simplifies us. He strips away what we thought we needed in order to show us what we truly need. Sometimes God allows the shaking because He loves you too much to let you rest your life on something that cannot last.

Thought provoking question: What has been shaking in your life lately, and could God be protecting you by removing what could not hold you?

3. Hope Carved in Stone

Hope is not merely an emotion that rises and falls with the day. Hope is an engraving. Feelings can shift like the weather, but an inscription in stone remains, even after the storm has passed. Hope is what God carves into the soul when life tries to chisel you down. It is not the fragile optimism of someone untouched by pain. It is the steady witness of someone held by the Rock.

When life cuts deep, the Rock holds the inscription of your faith. Every scar becomes a line in your testimony, not because suffering is good, but because God is faithful in the midst of it. I remember long nights when tears seemed to wash away my prayers, when words felt too heavy to carry and too small to matter. Yet even silence has a sound when it presses against faith's surface. Even the moments when nothing was said were still moments when something was being formed. God was not absent. He was carving endurance into the walls of my spirit, shaping a strength that could not be borrowed from applause, comfort, or convenience.

There are seasons when the Lord feels quiet, but quiet does not mean vacant. A surgeon is quiet during the work. Not because nothing is happening, but because something delicate is underway. A builder is focused, not noisy, while laying beams that must hold weight for years to come. In the same way, God may be doing deep work in you that does not announce itself until later. He may be strengthening the inner places you rarely see, reinforcing the foundation beneath your smile, and steadying your heart for what you will face down the road.

The Rock is forming something in you that will not crumble under tomorrow's pressure. He is inscribing patience where impatience used to rule. He is engraving humility where pride once tried to protect you. He is carving discernment where confusion used to live. The wounds may be real, and the ache may still linger, but God does not waste pain. He redeems it. He turns the very places you wanted erased into places of witness, where your life can one day say, with quiet authority, "I survived because God sustained me."

And when you look back, you may realize that what felt like a delay was actually depth. What felt like silence was steady work. What felt like breaking was, in God's hands, a shaping. The Rock was not watching your suffering from a distance. He was holding you close while He formed a hope that could not be shaken loose.

Thought-provoking question: What if the very pain you wanted God to erase is the place where He is engraving the strength you will one day need?

4. The Unshakable Lesson

To live anchored in Christ means learning how to rest even while rebuilding. You may be surrounded by uncertainty, but inside you can dwell in stability. When we stop fighting for control, we feel the quiet pulse of divine security. Hope no longer depends on the outcome. It depends on presence.

And presence changes everything. When God is your Rock, you do not have to panic when the wind rises. You can grieve without drowning. You can wait without falling apart. You can move forward without needing every answer first. Stability is not the absence of trouble. Stability is the presence of God beneath you.

Stillness is not inactivity, and it is not avoidance. Stillness is a sacred posture, a deliberate act of trust where striving ceases, and the heart gently transfers its weight to God. It is the quiet surrender of what we cannot manage into the hands of the One who never loses control. In seasons of upheaval, stillness becomes the place where God stabilizes the believer, not always by removing the storm, but by anchoring the soul so deeply that the storm cannot uproot what grace has secured.

We often equate faith with movement. We assume that if we are truly believing, we must be doing more, fixing faster, thinking harder, praying with greater intensity, and exhausting ourselves in the name of responsibility. But God often does His deepest work when human effort steps back. There are moments when the Lord, in His wisdom, calls us to stop reaching for the steering wheel and to release the pressure to manufacture outcomes. Stillness is not weakness. It is obedience. It is the quiet decision to trust God's governance when outcomes feel uncertain, and control feels necessary. It is the moment faith stops negotiating and starts resting, not because the situation has become simple, but because God has become sufficient.

In stillness, we learn to listen again. We begin to recognize that our anxious activity can be a form of self-protection, a way of trying to outrun fear. Yet the Lord is not impressed by our frantic labor, and He is not moved by our panic. He invites us into a holy pause where the soul becomes honest, and the spirit becomes receptive. Stillness does not deny the reality of the storm; it refuses to be ruled by it. It turns down the noise long enough to hear the steady voice of God, the voice that speaks peace without promising immediate change, the voice that says, "I am with you," even while the winds still blow.

God does not shame trembling faith. He does not demand composure before offering care. He does not stand at a distance until we look strong enough to be helped. Instead, He draws near and steadies us while we tremble. He strengthens what is frail, supports what is weary, and holds what feels like it might collapse. Stillness becomes the space where fear loosens its grip, not because answers arrive on our timetable, but because God's presence becomes more real than the threats around us. In that holy quiet, the heart discovers that it can breathe again, not because every question has been solved, but because it is no longer carrying what it was never meant to carry alone.

This is where faith matures. Not by rushing toward solutions, but by remaining present with God. Not by forcing doors open, but by waiting with confidence that God is already at work. In stillness, we learn that trust is not proved by speed, but by surrender. And as we rest there, steady and held, we begin to realize that the truest peace is not the absence of trouble. It is the settled assurance that the Lord is near, the Lord is faithful, and the Lord will finish what He has begun.

Question for the reader: Have you been standing on temporary ground, and how might God be inviting you to stand on Him again?

5. Graceful Flow Moment

Close your eyes for a moment and picture the Rivercess coastline. See the wide Atlantic breathing in and out, waves rolling forward to meet the land, and the land leaning into rock that has learned how to stand. Hear the wind moving across the shore like a gentle hymn, carrying a quiet song of peace. That is how grace meets the believer's heart. Grace is not hurried. It is steady. It comes again and again, like the tide, touching the places you thought were too worn to heal and too heavy to hold.

Watch the waves as they crash and retreat. They come with force, but they also return to their source. There is a holy rhythm in that. Let it speak to you. No matter how far the tide of circumstance seems to pull you, you will always be drawn back into God. You may feel stretched, but you are not severed. You may feel pressed, but you are not abandoned. The pull you feel is not proof that you are losing Him. It may be proof that He is still calling you, still gathering you, still holding your life within His reach.

Notice something else about that shoreline. The Rock does not repel the waves. He receives them and remains. The waters do not intimidate the Rock, and the Rock does not flinch when the surge arrives. He stands, not in resistance, but in permanence. That is a picture of God's grace. God does not panic when your emotions rise, when your questions crash in, or when your strength feels thin. He does not push you away because you are overwhelmed. He receives you. He holds the impact. He remains steady. Life may surge, but grace stands.

Some days, your soul feels like the ocean, restless and loud. Other days, it feels like the shoreline, tired from being hit again and again. But grace meets you in both places. It meets you in the crash and in the quiet. It meets you in the mess of what you cannot explain and the weary prayers you can barely form. Grace does not demand that you arrive polished. It invites you to come as you are, and then it begins to restore your sense of belonging. It reminds you that you are not drifting without a home. You have a Source. You have a Rock. You have a God who remains.

So let this be your gentle turning point today. Breathe deep. Let the sound of the waves become a reminder that God's mercy is not a one-time visit. It is a continual return. It comes to you, and it calls you back, again and again.

Thought-provoking question: Where have you been pushed by life's tides, and where is God inviting you to return to Him as your source?

6. Prayer of Renewed Strength

Lord, my Rock and my Redeemer, when the ground beneath me trembles and my thoughts begin to scatter, anchor my faith in You. When I feel the pull of fear, steady me with Your nearness. When my strength runs thin, hold me up with the quiet firmness of Your love. Teach me to trust the solid truth of Your promises more than the shifting feelings of my present pain. Help me remember that what I feel is real, but it is not final, and it does not define what You are doing in me.

Father, carve Your hope into the places that once broke. Touch the fractures I tried to hide, the disappointments I tried to carry alone, and the wounds that still ache when life presses in. Where bitterness attempted to take root, plant Your peace. Where shame tried to speak louder than grace, let Your mercy rise like morning light. Where my heart has learned to brace for impact, teach it to rest in Your steadiness. Do not merely give me relief for a moment, Lord. Give me renewal from the inside out.

Strengthen my spirit to stand, not with stubborn pride, but with humble confidence in You. Train my soul to lean on You without apology. Quiet my need to control outcomes and replace it with trust in Your wisdom. When I cannot see the way forward, let Your Word become a lamp in the dark. When my prayers feel small, and my voice feels weak, hear me still, and remind me that You are close to the brokenhearted and faithful to the weary.

Lord, make my life living evidence that Your foundation never cracks. Let my steady steps testify that You are the Rock beneath every season. Let my endurance preach when my mouth is silent. Let my peace be a witness that You are present, even in the storm. And when the shaking comes, keep me from collapsing into despair. Root me deeper. Establish me stronger. Hold me close until I can breathe again, and then lead me forward with renewed strength, courage, and joy.

In the name of Jesus Christ, my Savior and my sure foundation, amen.

7. Affirmation and Grace Reminder

I am rooted in the Living Rock.

I am steadied by God, not shaken by circumstance. When life shifts under my feet and the winds rise without warning, I do not belong to panic. I belong to the One who remains. I am held beneath every season, beneath joy and sorrow, beneath gain and loss, beneath clarity and confusion. The world may move, but God does not. His faithfulness is not a passing wave. It is a deep foundation.

I trust what God is building, even when I cannot see it. I trust His hidden work, His quiet strengthening, His careful shaping. I may not understand the timing, but I do not doubt the Builder. I may not see the full picture, but I know the Rock under me is sure. And because He is steady, I can breathe. Because He is faithful, I can wait. Because He is present, I can stand.

Now pause here.

Do not rush past this moment. Let your soul become still before God. Lay down the need to explain everything. Release the pressure to fix everything. Sit quietly in His presence and let the Holy Spirit search the deeper places with gentleness and truth.

Ask yourself, slowly and honestly:

What have I been leaning on that cannot hold me?
Where is God inviting me to rest instead of strive?

Consider these questions in the quiet of your heart:

1. What am I leaning on that God may be asking me to release?

2. Where have I felt God steady me even while I was still trembling?

3. If I truly trusted God as my Rock, what fear would lose its grip today?

And let this Word settle over you like a calm covering:

"The LORD shall fight for you, and ye shall hold your peace."
Exodus 14:14 (KJV)

CHAPTER 2 – WHEN FAITH MEETS FEAR

Trusting God in the Shadows of Uncertainty

Fear does not always arrive with loud panic or trembling hands. More often, it slips in quietly, dressed in respectable clothing. It comes disguised as responsibility, caution, or realism. It speaks in reasonable tones and asks believable questions: What if this fails? What if God does not come through this time? What if you are mistaken? Fear rarely announces itself as an open opponent of faith. Instead, it presents itself as wisdom detached from trust, offering careful logic without the comfort of God's presence. It sounds prudent, even mature, yet it subtly moves the heart from resting in God to rehearsing worst-case scenarios.

It is important to understand that faith and fear often occupy the same space. Their meeting is not a sign of spiritual failure. It is evidence that something meaningful is at stake. Where purpose is present, resistance is often near. Where obedience matters, anxiety will try to speak. Faith does not disappear when fear shows up. Faith is tested, refined, and revealed. The presence of fear does not cancel faith. It simply exposes what we truly believe about God's character when the outcome is unclear.

This chapter begins with a simple, freeing truth: believing God does not require the absence of fear. It requires obedience in the presence of fear. Faith is not the refusal to feel. It is the decision to follow God even while the heart is still learning to be steady. It is choosing to pray when worry is loud, choosing to take the next right step when certainty is unavailable, choosing to trust God's voice over fear's questions. Mature faith is not fearless. Mature faith is anchored.

And God does not withdraw when fear arises. He remains near, steady, and attentive. He does not turn away because you feel anxious, nor does He demand perfect composure before He offers His care. He is the Shepherd who stays close when the valley grows dark, the Father who strengthens trembling hands, the Rock who does not shift when the ground feels unstable. The shadows of uncertainty do not signal God's departure. They reveal the places where trust must deepen beyond what is visible or familiar. In those very places, God invites us to move from merely believing in His power to resting in His faithfulness, not because we can predict the outcome, but because we know the One who holds it.

There are nights when the air feels heavy and the heart trembles with what ifs. The room is quiet, but your thoughts are loud. You pray, yet heaven feels silent. You believe, yet the road ahead is dark. And it is in those very moments, not in the bright hours of clarity, that faith and fear collide. The collision is not always dramatic. Sometimes it is subtle, like a slow pressure on the chest. Sometimes it is sudden, like a wave of dread at the sound of a phone call or the sight of a bill. Either way, the encounter reveals something important. It tests whether the Word you confess truly lives inside you, and whether your trust is rooted in God's character or in your circumstances.

This chapter exists for the believer who is standing in the shadows, not because God has moved, but because life has changed. It is written for the person who feels uncertain and yet still wants to be faithful. It is for the heart that says, I love God, but I am afraid. It is for the soul learning that courage is not the absence of fear. Courage is obedience while fear is present. The purpose of this chapter is to call you back to the living truth that God is near even when you cannot feel Him, and that His promises remain firm even when your emotions are shaking.

I remember standing in a season where everything familiar was shaken. The plans I held close suddenly made no sense. Doors I expected to open stayed shut. Answers I thought would come quickly did not come at all. Fear told me quietly that I had forgotten, that perhaps my prayers had lost their power. But deep inside, faith kept knocking, softly yet steadily, reminding me that God's presence is not measured by my comfort, but by His unchanging promise. That is one of the sacred lessons of uncertainty. God does not stop being faithful because life becomes unclear. He does not stop being God because the future feels hidden.

Faith is not always loud. It does not always shout over fear. Sometimes faith simply stands. It stands when the diagnosis comes. It stands when the door closes. It stands when you cannot see tomorrow but choose to trust anyway. Faith stands like a lamp in a windy place. The flame flickers, but it remains. It remains because the source is not human strength. The source is divine grace.

The beauty of divine faith is that it never denies fear's existence. It simply refuses fear the final word. Fear may enter the room, but it cannot stay once faith begins to worship. Worship invites light, and light always exposes the lies that darkness says. Fear tells you God is absent. Worship reminds you of His faithfulness. Fear tells you you are alone. Worship declares that the Lord is with you. Fear tells you it is over. Worship lifts its eyes and says; God is still writing.

Every person of destiny must meet fear at some point. Fear is often the threshold that separates the ordinary from the anointed. It is the gate you walk through when you are about to grow. Fear says you cannot. Faith replies God already did. Fear says you will fall. Faith says the everlasting arms are underneath you. Fear says this is too much. Faith says His grace is sufficient.

When I chose to surrender the unknown to God, I discovered something sacred. Peace does not mean understanding. Peace means trusting while you wait for the understanding. Peace is not the absence of questions. Peace is the presence of God holding you steady while questions remain. There is a quiet strength that comes when you stop demanding that tomorrow explain itself, and you simply rest in the One who holds tomorrow.

Faith Reflection

Faith is not measured by how calm you feel, but by how willing you are to remain faithful when calm is unavailable. There are moments when peace feels out of reach, when the heart is restless, the mind is crowded, and the future seems wrapped in fog. In those moments, it is easy to assume we are failing spiritually because we do not feel steady. Yet Scripture teaches us that genuine trust is not proven by the absence of pressure. It is proven by obedience under pressure. When you continue to follow God while your emotions are still catching up, you are not weak. You are growing.

Obedience in the midst of strain is one of the clearest expressions of trust. Anyone can praise when the path is bright and the answers are immediate. But faith is refined when the road is hard, when prayers feel unanswered, and when the soul must lean on God's character rather than visible evidence. Faith does not always shout victory. Sometimes it whispers endurance. Sometimes it simply keeps showing up. It keeps praying. It keeps loving. It keeps forgiving. It keeps choosing what is right, even when doing so feels costly. This is not a lesser faith. This is a deeper faith.

There are seasons when faith stands quietly, holding its ground without reassurance, without applause, and without clarity. It does not demand to understand everything before it obeys. It does not bargain with God for certainty before it will take the next step. This kind of faith is not built on emotional confidence. It is built on the nature of God Himself. It says, "I do not see the whole picture, but I know the One who does." It says, "I cannot explain the timing, but I trust the heart of my Father." It says, "My feelings may be shaking, but my foundation is sure." When faith chooses obedience while fear is still present, it matures beyond feelings and becomes rooted in truth.

And here is the tenderness of God: He honors obedience offered with trembling hands. He does not require perfect courage before He calls you forward. He does not wait until your voice is strong before He receives your prayer. He meets you in weakness, strengthens you in process, and walks with you as you learn to trust. The Lord is not repelled by your trembling. He is drawn to your dependence. A willing heart matters to Him. A surrendered yes matters to Him. He responds to trust that is honest, even if it is not yet confident.

Faith that remains, even when uncertain, carries weight in heaven. It is precious to God because it reflects His worth. It declares that He is trustworthy, not only when life is smooth, but when life is hard. It reveals a love that is not based on convenience, and a devotion that is not driven by emotion alone. So, if you are in a season where calm is unavailable, do not condemn yourself. Instead, bring your heart to God as it is, and let your obedience be your offering. Keep your hand in His. Keep your feet moving in His direction. Keep your life aligned with His Word. Your faith is speaking, even in whispers, and heaven hears it.

"The Lord will fight for you; you need only to be still."
Exodus 14:14

This verse does not tell you that battles will never come. It tells you that God does not leave you to fight alone. It calls you into a posture that feels difficult when your heart is racing. Stillness. Trust. Surrender. Stillness is not passivity. Stillness is a holy decision to stop wrestling in your own strength and to let God take the weight. There are seasons when the Lord instructs you to move, but there are also seasons when the most powerful act of faith is to be still and let God defend, guide, and deliver.

And there is another Scripture that steadies us when fear tries to speak louder than faith.

"Be still, and know that I am God."
Psalm 46:10

To be still is to remember who God is. It is to let His sovereignty silence your panic. It is to let His presence calm your nervous thoughts. It is to return to the truth that He is God even when you do not understand the path.

Prayer of Trust in Uncertainty

Lord my God,
when fear rises in my chest like a sudden tide and clarity fades like light at dusk, teach me to trust You beyond what I can see. When my mind runs ahead of me, rehearsing every worst case scenario, draw me back into the safety of Your presence. When uncertainty feels loud and relentless, remind me that You are not confused, You are not delayed, and You are not distant. You are the same God who sees the end from the beginning, and You hold my life with steady hands.

Our glorious Father, quiet the voices that magnify uncertainty. Silence the inner accusations that say I am alone, that I have failed, that nothing will change. Still the anxious thoughts that keep circling like restless birds, never landing, never letting me rest. Teach me to discern between wisdom and fear, between caution and unbelief, between careful planning and spiritual panic. Let Your Word become the strongest voice in my heart. Let Your Spirit speak peace where my emotions demand proof.

Anchor my heart in Your faithfulness. When I cannot trace Your hand, help me trust Your heart. When the path is unclear, let Your promises be my footing. When my feelings shake, be the Rock beneath me. Forgive me for the times I try to control what I should surrender. Forgive me for measuring Your goodness by my comfort, and Your timing by my impatience. Wash me with the quiet assurance that You are working, even when I cannot see the movement.

Lord, help me obey even when courage feels thin and faith feels stretched. Strengthen me to take the next right step, not because I feel strong, but because You are strong. Give me grace to do what You have asked of me today, not with perfection, but with sincerity. Teach me that obedience is not the reward of confidence, it is the fruit of trust. Hold my trembling hands, steady my wavering thoughts, and keep my feet from sliding into despair.

Today, I choose trust over panic. I will not be ruled by what might happen. I will be guided by what You have already spoken. I choose worship over worry. I will lift my eyes above the storm and fix them on the One who cannot be moved. I choose stillness over control. I release my grip on outcomes, and I place my heart, my family, my plans, my future, and my unanswered questions into Your care.

Lord, breathe Your peace into the places where my soul feels crowded. Cover me with the calm strength of Your presence. Restore my joy where anxiety has drained it. Renew my hope where disappointment has bruised it. And if the answers do not come quickly, let Your presence be enough. If the door does not open today, let Your promise steady me. If the storm does not pass immediately, let Your grace keep me standing.

You are faithful. You have been faithful. You will be faithful.
I rest in You, my Rock and my Redeemer. In Jesus' name, Amen.

Reflection Guide and Grace Journal

"The Lord will fight for you; you need only to be still."
Exodus 14:14

"Be still, and know that I am God."
Psalm 46:10

Affirmations

I trust God even when fear is present. My feelings may tremble, but my foundation is sure. I obey even when the path is unclear. God guides my steps, and His wisdom is greater than my sight. I am held by God in uncertain seasons. I am not drifting, and I am not alone. Faith remains alive within me. It may be quiet, but it is steady, and it is growing.

Silent Reflection

Pause here.
Breathe slowly and deeply. Let your shoulders relax. Let your heart settle.

Where has fear tried to speak the ending of your story? What conclusion has anxiety been whispering, as if it has authority over your future?

Now listen for a better voice.
Where is God inviting you to trust Him instead?

Remain still for a moment.
Not striving. Not arguing. Just resting before God.

Let faith answer fear, not with frantic words, but with steady trust.

Silent Reflection (Heart Held, Not Written)

Settle your heart for a moment. Let the noise inside you soften. Breathe slowly, and remember that God is near, even here.

• Where has fear been trying to write the ending of your story, and how is God calling you to trust Him instead?
• What would it look like to worship in the very place you have been worrying?
• Are you demanding answers from God, or learning to rest in His character while you wait?
• What lie has darkness been whispering, and what truth from Scripture will you speak back?

Grace Journal

Write freely below. Do not perform. Do not polish. Be honest. Be tender. Let your pen become a prayer, and let your words tell the truth you have been carrying.

Then return to these Scriptures until they settle in your spirit like a calm covering:

"The LORD shall fight for you, and ye shall hold your peace."
— Exodus 14:14 (KJV)

"Be still, and know that I am God."
— Psalm 46:10 (KJV)

CHAPTER 3 – THE POWER OF STILL BELIEVING

The Power of Still Believing: When Hope Refuses to Die

There are moments in life when faith feels less like a victorious march and more like a quiet stance in the middle of a storm. Sometimes faith is not about moving mountains. It is about standing still when everything in you wants to run. It is about waking up on the thirteenth disappointment, tasting the familiar sting of delay, and still finding the strength to say, "I still believe."

That sentence may look small on paper, but it carries the weight of a battlefield. It is not the language of people who have never been wounded. It is the voice of a heart that has been pressed, stretched, and tested, yet refuses to let go of God. Still believing is not naïve. It is sacred courage. It is the whisper of a soul that has seen pain close up, that has watched dreams stagger, that has endured unanswered prayers, and yet still expects God's goodness.

Some people think hope is only for the light. But true hope learns to breathe in darkness. True hope is not the denial of what hurts. It is the decision to trust God in the presence of what hurts. And that is why still believing is powerful. Because it says, "This is real, and I am still here. This is heavy, and I am still holding on. This is unclear, and I am still trusting the One who sees."

Every promise worth holding will pass through the fire of delay. It will be tested not only by opposition, but by time. Not only by enemies, but by waiting. And waiting is not gentle. Waiting can feel like a slow ache in the chest. It can feel like watching the calendar turn while your prayer stays in the same place. It can feel like standing at a door that will not open, trying to interpret silence without losing your peace.

Yet the fire does not come to destroy you. It comes to purify your conviction. It comes to burn away shaky motives, frantic striving, and the need to control outcomes. It comes to teach your faith how to stand without props. It comes to make you the kind of believer who can still praise when the proof has not arrived yet.

I remember sitting in silence, watching years of effort seem to vanish. I had prayed, fasted, and waited, yet heaven appeared quiet. My heart wanted to interpret that quiet as rejection. My thoughts wanted to call it failure. But in that silence, God was shaping me. The lesson was not only in getting what I asked for. The lesson was in learning that His timing protects what His love intends to preserve.

That is a truth you rarely learn in comfort. You learn it in the long pause. You learn it when you have done all you know to do, and the next instruction from heaven is not "run," but "rest." Not "push," but "trust." Not "figure it out," but "hold your peace."

Scripture gives language to this holy posture. It speaks it plainly, without apology.

"The Lord will fight for you; you need only to be still."
Exodus 14:14

These words were not written for people lounging in ease. They were spoken to people trapped between danger and the unknown. Behind them was bondage. In front of them was a sea. Panic was reasonable. Fear was loud. Yet God's instruction was not frantic motion. It was stillness. Not because the battle was small, but because God was present. Not because the threat was imaginary, but because deliverance was already in His hands.

Still believing means trusting that the Author of your story knows every hidden page. It means believing that God's pen has not slipped. It means remembering that the chapter you are in is not the final chapter, even if it feels like the longest chapter. The pause is not punishment. The pause is preparation.

There are pauses that protect you. There are delays that save you from receiving something too early, before your character can carry it, before your heart can steward it, before your life can hold it without breaking. God does not only prepare blessings. He prepares people. He does not only open doors. He strengthens knees, steadies minds, and purifies motives so that when the door opens, the blessing does not crush you.

Each "not yet" is a divine pause before a better unveiling. Each tear is a hidden seed of testimony. Many people only honor the harvest, but heaven also honors the seed. Heaven honors the tears that watered the ground when you could not see growth. Heaven honors the nights you prayed with a tired voice and still meant every word. Heaven honors the days you showed up again, not because you felt strong, but because you refused to quit on God.

Still believing does not always look like shouting. Sometimes it looks like getting out of bed when your soul feels bruised. Sometimes it looks like worshiping with trembling hands. Sometimes it looks like doing the next right thing while your heart is still healing. Still believing is the quiet strength of a person who has learned that God is faithful even when life is confusing.

When faith matures, it no longer needs proof. It only needs presence. You stop demanding that God prove Himself according to your schedule. You stop measuring His love by how quickly things change. You stop insisting on understanding before you obey. Something deeper begins to grow in you. You realize you do not just want what God can give. You want God Himself. You stop asking God to show you the way because you finally realize He is the way.

And this is where hope becomes unkillable. Because hope anchored in outcomes is fragile, but hope anchored in God is firm. Outcomes shift. People shift. Seasons shift. But God does not shift. When your hope rests in His character, hope refuses to die because God refuses to fail.

There is a sacred kind of worship that rises only from disappointment. It is not the worship of those who got everything they wanted quickly. It is the worship of those who waited, wept, questioned, and still bowed. It is the worship that says, "Lord, I do not understand, but I trust You." It is the worship that declares, "My faith is not for sale, and my hope is not negotiable." There are seasons when faith no longer feels strong, loud, or victorious. You still pray, but the excitement that once carried your words faded. You still believe, yet the emotion that once fueled your confidence has grown quiet. Worship may feel heavier than it used to, and the promises you once declared with ease may now be spoken with a trembling voice. But hear this clearly. This is not the death of faith. This is the place where still believing begins.

Still believing is not dramatic. It does not announce itself with bold certainty or visible triumph. It does not always come with goosebumps, tears, or a sudden rush of courage. Still believing is quieter than that. It is the steady decision to remain when nothing seems to be reinforcing your trust. It is staying with God when you do not feel carried by joy, when circumstances have not yet shifted, and when the heart has learned what it feels like to wait. It is waking up after repeated disappointment and choosing God again, not because you have guarantees, but because you know who He is. It is faith that refuses to let go even when the soul feels tired.

This kind of faith does not draw its strength from visible progress. It is not sustained by quick results or obvious breakthroughs. It draws strength directly from God. It leans on His character when the evidence feels thin. It depends on His faithfulness when the future looks uncertain. Still believing says, "Lord, I do not understand, but I will not walk away." It says, "I do not feel strong, but I will keep my hand in Yours." It says, "I have questions, but I will not surrender my trust to fear." This is not shallow faith. This is deep faith. This is faith that has been stripped of theatrics and purified by endurance.

The power of still believing lies not in movement, but in remaining. It is faith that stays when answers do not come quickly, when relief delays, and when hope feels thin, but not gone. It is the quiet courage to keep showing up. It is the holy endurance that holds its ground in the dark, trusting that God is still God even when the night is long. Sometimes the greatest testimony is not what you overcame in a moment, but what you refused to quit overtime.

So, if you are in that season now, do not despise it. Do not interpret the quietness as failure. Do not measure your faith by how energized you feel. Measure it by your willingness to remain. God sees the prayers you whisper. He sees the obedience you offer without applause. He sees your persistence when nothing is easy. And He honors faith that stays. In the sacred place of still believing, God is doing a work that will not easily unravel. He is making you steady. He is teaching you to trust Him for Himself. And in time, what feels like quiet endurance today will become a living witness tomorrow that the Lord held you, even when you could barely hold on.

Faith Reflection

Believing again after disappointment is one of life's highest forms of worship. It says, "My faith is not for sale, and my hope is not negotiable." It is the spiritual stance of a heart that refuses to let pain become the final prophet. It is the holy decision to allow God's promise to speak louder than your present circumstances.

If you are still waiting, hold your position. God does some of His best work in the dark. Many of His greatest miracles begin in hidden places. Roots grow where eyes cannot see. Seeds break open underground before they ever rise above ground. In the same way, God may be working in your life in ways you cannot measure yet. Do not mistake hidden work for absent work.

Your stillness is not emptiness. It is expectancy. It is the posture that says, "I know God is moving even if I cannot see the movement." It is the confidence that God can fight battles beyond human reach. It is the quiet assurance that heaven is not nervous.

And when the dawn breaks, your faith will prove it never died in the night.

"The Lord will fight for you; you need only to be still."
Exodus 14:14

Let that verse become your resting place. Let it calm the places in you that keep trying to control what only God can handle. Let it silence the urge to rush ahead of grace. Let it strengthen you when waiting feels like weakness. Stillness in God is not giving up. Stillness in God is giving over. It is placing your life back into the hands that formed you.

So today, if hope feels bruised but not broken, speak it again, even if your voice shakes: "I still believe." If all you have is a whisper, let the whisper rise. Heaven hears whispers. If all you have is a tear, let the tear fall. God counts tears. If all you have is stillness, hold that stillness with reverence. Stillness is sometimes the strongest faith you can offer.

And when fear tries to bury your expectation, remember this. Hope does not die where God is present. Hope does not die where God has spoken. Hope does not die where God is working.

There are moments when faith is reinforced by answered prayer, visible growth, or the encouragement of others. In those seasons, belief feels bright. It feels supported. It feels easier to keep going because something outside of you seems to echo what you already hold inside. But there are also seasons when none of those reinforcements are present. The prayers are still offered, yet the answers seem delayed. The desire to obey remains, yet the outward signs feel faint. In such seasons, still believing is the faith that continues when reinforcement disappears.

This kind of faith is costly because it offers no immediate reward. It receives no applause. It lives without reassurance. It does not get the quick relief that makes endurance feel worth it. Yet it is powerful because it rests entirely on God's character rather than on circumstances. When faith no longer feeds on outcomes, it learns to survive on truth. It learns to say, "God is good," not because life is easy, but because God is faithful. It learns to trust the heart of God when the hand of God is not yet visible.

God values this faith deeply. It proves that trust is not conditional. It demonstrates that belief has matured beyond transaction and into relationship. It shows that you are not holding onto God only for what He gives, but because of who He is. Still believing is love that remains, devotion that stays, and loyalty that does not evaporate when the season turns hard.

Remaining When Explanations Disappear

Still believing requires learning how to remain when explanations are absent. God does not always explain Himself, not because He is distant, but because He is developing depth. Understanding was never meant to carry the full weight of your faith. God was. The Lord knows the human heart often tries to reduce pain by solving it, but some seasons cannot be solved. They can only be walked through with God.

When explanations fade, faith is forced to choose its foundation. Will it rest on logic, or will it rest on God? Still believing releases the pressure to interpret every delay and untangle every mystery. It chooses to stay connected to God within the season instead of standing outside the season demanding a reason. Remaining is not stagnation. It is endurance in motion beneath the surface, the slow strengthening of roots while the ground above looks unchanged.

Faith as Quiet Resistance

Still believing is also an act of quiet resistance. It resists despair without shouting hope. It resists fear without demanding certainty. It resists quitting without pretending strength. This faith does not deny pain or disappointment. It simply refuses to let them write the ending. It refuses to let a difficult chapter become the final word.

Heaven honors this resistance because it depends on God rather than self-confidence. Quiet faith carries great spiritual weight. God sees the believer who stays when leaving would feel easier. He sees the one who keeps praying when prayer feels like labor, who keeps loving when love feels costly, who keeps obeying when obedience feels unrewarded. That staying becomes testimony, not only to people, but before heaven itself.

Staying Is Not Weakness

Staying is often misunderstood. To some, it can look like inaction. But in the spiritual realm, it is strength. Still believing requires patience, humility, and trust, qualities that are formed slowly and deeply. God does not rush this process. He works beneath the surface, strengthening roots that will later support visible fruit. Faith that remains becomes resilient. It learns how to survive long seasons without collapsing. It becomes steadier, less dependent on emotion, and more anchored in God's promises.

Staying with God when faith feels quiet is one of the strongest acts of obedience. It is the decision to keep your heart turned toward Him, even when you cannot feel the warmth of the sun.

Unseen Growth in Still Believing

Growth does not always feel like progress. Sometimes it feels like endurance. Still believing develops spiritual depth that quick victories cannot produce. It forms humility, compassion, and a stronger dependency on God. It teaches you to see others with tenderness because you know what it is to wait, to ache, and to keep trusting anyway.

This growth often goes unnoticed, but it is essential. When faith has learned how to remain, it becomes unshakable. The believer who has practiced still believing is not easily moved by delay or disappointment. God does deep work in seasons that feel uneventful, and what seems like slow days are often the days when He is building lasting strength.

Reflection on Long Obedience

There are believers who have obeyed for a long time without visible reward. They have prayed faithfully, waited patiently, and trusted consistently. Over time, faith may feel quieter, not weaker, but more tender. This tenderness is not failure. It is evidence of endurance. It is the soft strength that comes from staying with God through many nights and realizing that His presence is enough to carry you.

God honors those who remain faithful even when obedience becomes costly. Long obedience shapes faith into something refined and lasting, a faith that does not need constant confirmation to survive. It is the kind of faith that can stand in the dark and still say, with steady truth, "I am here, Lord. I will not let go."

Prayer for Still Believing

Lord,
teach me how to remain when answers delay and strength feels thin. When my prayers feel repeated and my results feel slow, keep my heart from slipping into discouragement. Help me trust You without reinforcement, believe without explanation, and stay when it would be easier to leave. When my mind demands proof and my emotions crave relief, anchor me in the quiet certainty of who You are.

Father, steady my faith in Your character, not in what I can see. When progress feels invisible, remind me that Your work is not absent, only hidden. When the door does not open yet, help me wait without resentment. When I feel tired of hoping, breathe fresh endurance into my spirit. Teach me to love You for Yourself, not only for what You give, and to remain close even when the season feels silent.

Today, I choose still believing. I choose to keep my hand in Yours. I choose to obey in small ways, to worship in quiet ways, and to trust You in unseen ways. Hold me, strengthen me, and keep me rooted in the Living Rock.

In Jesus' name,
Amen.

Affirmations

I remain faithful even when faith feels quiet.
I trust God beyond what I understand.
My belief is rooted in truth, not outcomes.
Still believing carries power.

Silent Reflection

Pause here.
Do not hurry.
Breathe slowly and let your heart settle before God.

Where have you continued trusting God without reinforcement?
What strength has God been forming quietly within you?

Remain.
Let still believing hold you.

Silent Reflection (Heart Held, Not Written)

• Where in my life is God asking me to keep believing even without visible evidence?
• What delay may be protecting me rather than denying me?
• What does stillness look like for me in this season?

Grace Journal

Write freely below. Be honest with God. Be gentle with yourself. Let your words come as they are, without fear and without performance. Then return again to this promise until it settles in your spirit:

"The Lord will fight for you; you need only to be still."
Exodus 14:14

CHAPTER 4 – WHEN PURPOSE FEELS PAINFUL

The Breaking that Builds You

Purpose is a beautiful word, until it starts to hurt.

At first, purpose feels like a sunrise in the soul. It stirs vision, awakens courage, and makes you believe your life is headed somewhere holy. Purpose speaks in the language of destiny, calling, impact, and fruit. It paints pictures in your heart that you can almost touch. Yet there comes a point, often sooner than we expect, when purpose stops sounding like poetry and starts feeling like pressure.

Because purpose is not only a promise. Purpose is a process.

And sometimes that process is painful.

Many imagine that divine purpose feels like constant favor. They picture open doors, easy transitions, uninterrupted momentum, and endless applause. But often, purpose feels like being broken open in private while still called to lead in public. It feels like smiling while your soul is sore. It feels like serving while you are silently bleeding. It feels like carrying a word from God in one hand and carrying disappointment in the other, trying not to drop either one.

That is why this chapter exists. Not to glorify pain, but to interpret it. Not to celebrate suffering, but to reveal the sacred meaning that God can weave into it. The purpose of this chapter is to strengthen the believer who is walking through a season that feels like breaking, to comfort the heart that wonders if pain means abandonment, and to remind you that God often builds His strongest servants in places no one else can see.

Purpose Presses Before It Produces

When purpose begins to press you, it is not punishment. It is process.

There are pressures that destroy, and there are pressures that develop. There are weights that crush, and there are weights that strengthen. God does not press you to harm you. He presses you to shape you. The pressing exposes what is inside you. It reveals what is stable and what is surface. It shows you where your faith is rooted and where it has only been resting lightly on comfort.

God uses discomfort to reveal direction. He uses strain to refine focus. He allows pruning not because you are barren, but because you are about to bear more fruit.

Pruning is a tender mercy that often does not feel tender. It can feel like losing what you thought you needed. It can feel like doors closing that you prayed would stay open. It can feel like people fading from your life when you expected them to stay. It can feel like God is subtracting when you asked Him to add. But pruning is not the end of a tree. Pruning is the preparation of a tree. The branch that is cut is not being punished. It is being positioned for greater fruitfulness.

And yes, it hurts. Because growth stretches. And stretching can feel like tearing before it feels like strengthening.

When Pain Feels Like Rejection

There was a time I mistook pain for rejection. I thought perhaps God had moved on from my story. I looked at the ache, the delay, the closed doors, and I interpreted them as proof that heaven had changed its mind. Fear whispered, "Maybe you misunderstood your calling." Doubt leaned close and said, "Maybe you are not as chosen as you thought." And in the quiet hours, when there was no crowd, no platform, no applause, just me and God, the question rose like a heavy cloud: "Lord, why does purpose hurt like this?"

But what I later learned is this. The pain of purpose is often the proof of preparation.

Not all pain is holy, but God can redeem pain into holiness. Not all suffering is chosen by God, but God can turn suffering into training. And when He does, the pain becomes a sign that something is being formed in you that cannot be formed in comfort.

The anointing does not come cheaply. It is birthed through tears, endurance, and the surrender of what you thought you needed most. God does not only anoint gifts. He anoints vessels. He strengthens hearts. He steadies motives. He purifies character. He teaches you how to carry what you prayed for without being crushed by it.

Some blessings are too heavy for an unprepared spirit. Some assignments require a deeper foundation than you currently have. So God builds you. And building often begins with breaking.

Outgrowing What Used to Fit

When you are called, you will outgrow some seasons, friendships, and comforts. That is not cruelty. That is clarity. The call of God is not only about what you will do. It is about who you will become. And becoming often requires separation.

There are relationships that were right for one season but cannot travel with you into another. There are environments that once felt safe but now feel small. There are habits that once felt normal but now feel heavy. Purpose will not let you stay where you have outgrown. It will not let you keep pretending that less is enough. It will not let you keep clinging to what God is trying to release from your hands.

Every divine assignment carries a cost. Sometimes the cost is comfort. Sometimes the cost is familiarity. Sometimes the cost is being misunderstood. Sometimes the cost is obeying God when you would rather be approved by people. And sometimes the cost is learning how to walk alone with God in a way you never had to before.

But that cost cannot compare to the joy of seeing purpose fulfilled.

Because purpose is not pain forever. Purpose is pain with meaning. Purpose is pressure with promise. Purpose is the breaking that builds you.

The Sacredness of the Breaking

There is something sacred about the breaking.

It is in the breaking that oil flows. It is in the waiting that strength grows. And it is in the surrender that destiny finds you ready.

When God breaks us, He is not breaking our value. He is breaking our resistance. He is breaking the pride that would ruin us. He is breaking the dependence on human applause that would derail us. He is breaking the fear that would keep us small. He is breaking the old ways of thinking that cannot carry the future He is preparing.

Think of oil for a moment. Oil is not produced by gentle tapping. Oil comes through crushing, pressing, breaking. The olive does not become oil by remaining untouched. Something must happen to it. And in that pressing, what was hidden is released. What was trapped inside becomes nourishment, healing, light.

Some of the strongest believers you have ever met were not made in easy seasons. They were made in the pressing. They were formed in the furnace. They learned to pray when prayer felt dry. They learned to praise when praise cost them something. They learned to obey when obedience felt lonely. And through it all, they became people whose lives carry oil.

Stillness in the Middle of the Pain

This is where your faith is invited into a quieter strength, the strength of stillness.

"The Lord will fight for you; you need only to be still."
Exodus 14:14

Notice what God is saying. He is not denying the battle. He is promising His presence in it. He is not ignoring the threat. He is declaring His power over it. And then He gives an instruction that feels almost impossible when pain is loud. Be still.

Stillness does not mean you are doing nothing. Stillness means you are refusing to panic. Stillness means you are refusing to force what God has not released. Stillness means you are choosing trust over frenzy. It is the holy posture of a heart that says, "Lord, I will not ruin this season by trying to control it. I will let You fight. I will let You lead."

There are seasons when God calls you to take action. But there are also seasons when your most powerful act of faith is to be still, to let God do what only God can do, to let Him rearrange what you cannot fix, to let Him defend your name, your calling, your future.

"Be still, and know that I am God."
Psalm 46:10

That verse does not simply instruct your body. It ministers to your mind. It settles the soul that has been trying to figure everything out. It calls you back to the simplest, strongest truth: God is God. He is not uncertain. He is not confused. He is not threatened by your process. And He does not need you to understand everything in order for Him to be faithful.

Sometimes knowing God is not about gaining more information. It is about resting deeper in His character. It is learning that even when your life feels like a question mark, God remains the same.

Faith Reflection

If you are in a painful season, take heart. Heaven has not forgotten you. Pain is often the classroom of prophets, dreamers, and builders. You are not being buried. You are being planted.

The soil may feel dark, but new life is forming beneath the surface. The seed does not look alive when it is underground. It looks hidden. It looks silent. It looks forgotten. But it is not forgotten. It is being transformed. Something is happening that you cannot see yet.

Hold your peace. The same God who allowed the breaking is the One who will bring the beauty. The same hand that prunes is the hand that produces fruit. The same Lord who permits the process is the Lord who protects the promise.

And one day, when the season turns, you will look back and realize that what felt like breaking was building. What felt like loss was preparation. What felt like delay was protection. What felt like pain was purpose at work in you.

Still believing in the middle of this is not weakness. It is worship. It is courage. It is the quiet declaration that God is writing even when the page is hard.

Reflection Guide and Grace Journal

Reflecting on the Chapter, Rising Through the Storm

Use this space to pause, reflect, and record what God is speaking to your heart through this chapter.

1. What challenge taught you the true meaning of courage?
2. How did your faith carry you when everything else failed?
3. What promise from God are you holding onto today?

Grace Journal: Any thoughts?
Write freely. Let your heart speak. Let your pen become prayer.

Return again to these Scriptures and let them steady you:

"The Lord will fight for you; you need only to be still."
Exodus 14:14

"Be still, and know that I am God."
Psalm 46:10

CHAPTER 5 – GRACE IN THE WAITING ROOM

When God Seems Silent but Heaven Is Working

Waiting is rarely welcomed. It feels like an unexpected red light on a road you thought was finally opening up. It interrupts momentum, stretches expectations thin, and puts pressure on trust. And yet, in the life of faith, waiting is not a mistake. It is not a forgotten hallway in God's house. Waiting is often a designed season, measured out with intention and care, where the Lord tends to what cannot be rushed.

The waiting room is not empty space. It is supervised space. God does not leave His people unattended while they wait. He is not absent simply because the calendar has not turned the way you hoped. He is present, quietly governing what you cannot see, and faithfully holding what you are not yet ready to carry. The silence is not abandonment. The stillness is not neglect. Sometimes the very fact that you are waiting is evidence that God is working with precision, not panic.

Many assume that waiting means God has paused. But often, waiting means God is aligning timing, strengthening character, and protecting what is still forming. There are doors you are praying to walk through that would crush you if they opened too early. There are blessings that require maturity, not just desire. There are assignments that demand a heart anchored in God, not intoxicated by speed. What feels like delay can be mercy in disguise. What feels like "not yet" can be God's way of saying, "I'm building something deeper in you first."

Delay does not automatically signal denial. More often, it signals preparation. It is God preparing you and also preparing what you are about to step into. He is arranging people, shifting circumstances, closing off dangers you would have missed, and shaping the unseen framework beneath your future. You may feel stuck, but God may be setting. You may feel held back, but God may be holding you together.

And here is the tenderness of it: grace meets the believer in the waiting room. Not always to remove the tension, but to sustain the heart through it. Grace does not merely change circumstances, it strengthens souls. It teaches you how to breathe while you wait. How to worship with unanswered questions still on the table. How to stay soft without becoming fragile, and how to stay hopeful without becoming demanding.

Waiting also has a way of exposing what we rely on when movement stops. When you cannot "make it happen," waiting reveals where your confidence truly lives. It shows whether your faith is rooted in your schedule or in God's sovereignty, in your control or in His care. In the waiting room, the Lord gently confronts the need to rush, to force, to perform, to manipulate outcomes, and instead invites you into a steadier place. A place where faith does not depend on quick results but rests in the character of God.

Because waiting is not the same as resignation. Waiting, in its healthiest form, is active trust. It is patience with purpose. It is hope with humility. It is praying without panic, working without striving, and believing without demanding a deadline. In the waiting room, grace trains the heart to say, "Lord, I will not outrun You. I will not force what You have not formed. I will not trade Your best for my fastest."

So, if you find yourself waiting, do not assume you are wasting time. You may be in one of God's most sacred classrooms. The waiting room is where shallow faith becomes rooted faith. Where noisy anxiety is quieted into peace. Where the Lord teaches you that He is not only the God of the outcome, but the God of the process.

And when the door finally opens, you may discover something surprising: you did not just get through the waiting. The waiting, by grace, got something holy done in you.

Waiting is one of the most misunderstood seasons of life. It feels like delay, like a door left locked, like a clock moving without mercy. It can feel like life is happening to everyone else while you sit in the same place, holding the same prayer, carrying the same ache. But in heaven's language, waiting is not wasted time. Waiting is development. It is God's workshop, where what He promised is not only prepared for you, but you are prepared for what He promised.

When God asks you to wait, He is not denying you. He is designing you for a purpose that fits your needs and destiny.

There is a certain kind of grace that only grows in the waiting room. It is not the loud grace that celebrates quick victories. It is the quiet grace, the kind that learns to breathe without rushing, the kind that refuses to fold when nothing seems to move. It is the grace that holds steady when emotions rise and fall like waves. It is the grace that says, "Even here, God is still good. Even now, God is still working."

I have sat in that room before. It is not a room people choose. It is a room you enter when every door stays closed, when every plan unravels, when every prayer seems to echo back empty. In that room you begin to wonder if you heard God correctly. You begin to count the days and second guess your faith. You start rehearsing the same questions as a broken record: "Lord, where are You?" "Why is it taking so long?" "Did I miss You?" Yet, strangely, it is often in that silence that God is rearranging everything you cannot see.

Waiting often feels like God is doing nothing. But heaven is rarely still.

God may be silent in the ways you expected, yet active in ways you never imagined. He may not be answering with words, but He may be answering with alignment. He may be shifting people, closing wrong doors, protecting you from premature exposure, and strengthening your inner life so that when the promise arrives, you are not crushed by its weight. The waiting room is the place where God often removes what cannot hold you, heals what would hinder you, and refines what must become stronger.

Grace does not only sustain you. Grace shapes you.

Grace teaches you to see beauty in unfinished stories. It teaches you to trust that divine timing is never late. It teaches you to stop interpreting the pause as punishment. What feels like a pause is often the preservation of your promise. God is not postponing your good for pleasure. He is protecting your future with wisdom. He is keeping you from the heartbreak of receiving a blessing too early, before your roots are deep enough to carry it.

Because if God rushed your miracle, it might arrive without roots.

And a miracle without roots can fade as quickly as it comes. It can become a moment that does not last. But when God lets you wait, He is anchoring you for longevity. He is building spiritual muscles you will need in the next season. He is teaching you how to remain faithful when feelings are not cooperating. He is training your heart to seek Him more than the outcome. He is deepening your dependence so that your joy is not tied to speed, but to His presence.

The waiting room is not a place of punishment. It is a place of refinement.

Refinement is not comfortable. It is holy. It is the process that removes the weak mixtures from faith. It burns away impatience that would sabotage you. It exposes motives you did not know were there. It teaches you how to surrender control without surrendering hope. It stretches you until your trust becomes mature, steady, and unshakable.

And there is something else that happens in the waiting room. God becomes your portion. The blessings you want are still important, but you begin to realize that what you truly need is Him. Waiting has a way of stripping away the illusion that life is held together by your plans. It reminds you that God is the One who holds it all. He is the Rock beneath your feet, even when the ground feels uncertain.

Faith Reflection

Every divine promise has an appointed hour. Do not despise the waiting. Learn to worship there. The song you sing in delay will become the strength you stand on in destiny. Worship in the waiting room is not denial. It is defiance. It refuses to let delay turn into despair. It refuses to let silence become a sentence. It lifts its eyes and says, "God is still faithful, even here."

Waiting gracefully means believing that God's silence is not absence. It is strategy. It is the unseen construction of a miracle too big to be rushed. Sometimes the Lord does not respond quickly because He is building something carefully. He is forming a structure that will hold. He is laying foundation stones beneath your life that no one will praise, but your future will depend on.

So, breathe. Your lungs are not meant to live in panic. Your heart is not meant to be ruled by haste. Breathe and remember this. You are not forgotten. You are being fortified. You are not stuck. You are being strengthened. You are not delayed. You are being developed.

And when you feel your soul growing restless, return to the simple promise that steadies shaking hearts:

"The Lord will fight for you; you need only to be still."
Exodus 14:14

That Scripture is not a decoration. It is a lifeline. It tells you that the battle is not all on your shoulders. It reminds you that God does not ask you to wrestle your way into promise. Sometimes He asks you to be still, to stop striving, to stop frantic motion, and to trust that the same God who wrote the promise will also fulfill it.

Be still does not mean do nothing. It means do not panic. It means do not force. It means do not lose your peace trying to control what belongs to God. Stillness is trust with roots.

So, if you are in the waiting room today, hold your position. Let grace grow in you. Let faith deepen in you. Let worship rise from you. Heaven is working, even when you cannot see it.

Affirmations

- Waiting is not wasted. God is using this season with purpose.
- God is supervising what I cannot see and guiding what I cannot control.
- Grace sustains me while I wait, steadying my heart day by day.
- God's timing is not late. It is working for my good and His glory.

Silent Reflection

Pause here.
Breathe deeply.
Let your shoulders loosen. Let your spirit exhale.

Ask yourself gently:

- Where has waiting tested my trust and exposed my need to control?

- What might God be protecting me from, or preparing me for, through this delay?

Remain still.
Grace is at work, even when nothing seems to be moving.

Silent Reflection

Heart-held, not written

Sit quietly and consider what this waiting season may be shaping within you. Sometimes God is not speeding answers because He is strengthening trust. Sometimes the delay is not a wall, but a covering. Let your heart rest in who God is, not in how quickly things change.

Hold these questions with tenderness:

- What is God forming in me during this waiting season that could not be formed if everything moved quickly?

- Where am I being invited to trust God's timing more deeply rather than demanding immediate answers?

- **If my circumstances remain unchanged for a while, can my heart still rest confidently in who God is?**

Grace Journal

Use this space to pause, reflect, and gently name what God is stirring in your heart through this chapter.

Let honesty meet hope.
Let stillness become prayer.
Return again to this promise and allow it to steady you:

"The LORD shall fight for you, and ye shall hold your peace." *Exodus 14:14 (KJV)*

CHAPTER 6 – BE STILL AND KNOW

When Movement Stops but Miracles Begin

Stillness is not weakness. It is wisdom.

In a world that celebrates constant motion, stillness can feel like failure. We are trained to hurry, to fix, to explain, to respond. We are taught that if something is not changing, we must push harder. If a door will not open, we should knock louder. If the situation feels uncertain, we should gather more information, make more calls, and force more outcomes. Yet there are moments in the life of faith when God does not ask for more movement. He asks for more surrender. He asks for a sacred pause. He asks for a calm that is not rooted in circumstances, but in His sovereignty.

When life demands answers and heaven seems quiet, the instruction is often simple, and it comes like a steady hand on a trembling heart:

"Be still, and know that I am God."
Psalm 46:10

That Scripture is not a suggestion for calmer personalities only. It is a divine command for anxious seasons. It is the Lord calling your soul back from the edge. It is God saying, "Stop striving as though you are alone. Stop running as though your future depends only on your speed. Come back to Me. Remember who I am."

This is the essence of this chapter's title. "Be Still and Know" is not merely a phrase to decorate a wall. It is a spiritual posture that creates space for miracles. It is the moment movement stops, not because you have lost faith, but because you have chosen to place your faith in the One who does not need your panic to perform His power. This chapter is written to teach the heart what to do when you cannot control the timeline, cannot predict the outcome, and cannot fix what feels broken. It is written to show that stillness is often the doorway into divine alignment, where God begins the work you could never do with your own hands.

Stillness Is Not Doing Nothing

Stillness is one of the most misunderstood commands in Scripture. Many hear it and assume God is asking for passivity, hesitation, or retreat. But biblical stillness is not the absence of action. It is the presence of trust. To be still is to recognize God's authority precisely in those moments when your instinct is to act quickly, fix urgently, or control the outcome with your own hands.

Stillness confronts the human impulse to stay busy as proof of faithfulness. It challenges the subtle belief that movement always equals obedience, that doing more must mean trusting more. Yet God's command to be still is an invitation to pause long enough to remember who is truly in charge. In that holy pause, striving begins to loosen its grip, and trust quietly takes its rightful place.

Being still does not deny the storm. It does not pretend the wind is not howling or that the waters are not rising. Stillness simply declares that the storm does not outrank God. It confesses, with steady conviction, that what is happening around you is not greater than the One who holds you. And while your circumstances may be loud, stillness trains your soul to listen for the deeper voice beneath it all, the voice of the Lord who remains unshaken.

In the practice of stillness, fear is exposed and faith is strengthened. Anxiety is no longer allowed to lead the conversation. The heart learns to stop negotiating for control and starts yielding to God's care. Stillness becomes a form of worship, a quiet but courageous surrender that says, "Lord, I will not outrun You. I will not force what You have not formed. I will wait, not because I have no options, but because I trust Your wisdom more than my urgency."

It is why stillness is not weakness. It is spiritual strength under restraint. It is the decision to stand firm when everything in you wants to scramble. It is the sacred discipline of letting God be God, even when you would rather take the wheel. And in that posture, peace begins to rise, not because the storm has ended, but because your soul has remembered its Anchor.

Stillness does not mean doing nothing. It means refusing to panic while God performs what only He can do.

It is the sacred calm that comes when faith whispers, "Even now, God is working." It is not passivity. It is trust. It is not laziness. It is obedience. It is the decision to stop treating anxiety as if it were wisdom, and to start treating surrender as if it were strength.

There is a difference between rest and retreat. Stillness is not retreating from responsibility. It is retreating from striving. It is laying down the heavy belief that you must control everything to be safe. It is learning to trust that God can guide you even when your next step is unclear.

And yes, stillness can feel hard. Because stillness exposes what is inside us. When we are busy, we can hide from our fears. When we are moving, we can distract ourselves from our pain. But when we become still, we face the truth. We face the ache. We face the uncertainty. And in that honest place, God meets us, not with shame, but with grace.

When Striving Becomes a Substitute for Trust

Striving often wears the disguise of responsibility. On the surface, it looks admirable. It appears productive, disciplined, even spiritually mature. It stays busy, stays alert, stays "on top of things." But beneath constant striving, there is often a quieter motive at work: fear. Fear of delay. Fear of loss. Fear that if you loosen your grip, everything will fall apart. And when striving replaces trust, faith begins to feel like a performance to maintain rather than a relationship to live in.

The Lord never asked His people to carry what only He can manage. He never called you to be your own savior, your own provider, your own protector. Yet striving tries to secure outcomes without divine authority. It attempts to force timing, control people, and guarantee results through sheer effort. That kind of pressure drains the soul because it was never designed to be held by human strength. The heart grows weary not because it is working, but because it is working as if God is not present.

Stillness, by contrast, is not carelessness. It is surrender with confidence. It releases the burden of control and places it back where it belongs, in the hands of a faithful God. Stillness does not stop you from doing what is yours to do. It simply frees you from trying to do what is not yours to do. It teaches you to move in obedience without moving in anxiety, to labor with faith instead of fear.

Recognizing striving as counterfeit trust is the first step toward true rest. It is the moment the soul tells the truth: "I have been trying to manage what only God can govern." And in that honest confession, grace meets you. The Lord begins to untie the knots of urgency, calm the inner noise, and restore your heart to its rightful posture, not clenched in control, but open in trust.

There were seasons in my life when everything seemed to fall apart. I prayed, fasted, cried, and waited, yet heaven seemed to hold its peace. Plans unraveled. Relationships shifted. Doors closed. And the hardest part was not simply the disruption. The hardest part was the silence that followed the prayer.

It was there I discovered the difference between striving and surrendering. God was not asking me to try harder. He was asking me to trust deeper.

Striving says, "If I push enough, I can make this happen."
Surrender says, "If God has spoken, He will perform it."
Striving runs ahead because it is afraid of losing time.
Surrender waits because it believes God is never late.
Striving keeps grabbing for control.
Surrender opens its hands and says, "Lord, lead me."

This is where many believers wrestle. We love God, but we fear waiting. We believe, but we want timelines. We pray, but we want immediate evidence. And when evidence does not come quickly, we can begin to move from faith into friction, from trust into tension, from obedience into anxiety dressed up as effort.

Yet God often protects us from our own rushing. Sometimes the closed door is not God denying you. Sometimes it is God guarding you. Sometimes the delay is not God withholding.

Sometimes it is God preparing. And sometimes the silence is not God ignoring you. Sometimes it is God inviting you to stillness, because in stillness you learn to hear Him again.

Stillness Makes Room for Divine Alignment

When you choose stillness, you make room for divine alignment.

He cannot fix what you keep forcing. He cannot lead when you keep running ahead. And He cannot fill hands that refuse to let go.

There are things God desires to heal in us that cannot be healed while we are frantic. There are lessons He wants to teach that cannot be learned at full speed. There are doors He wants to open that we might miss if we keep sprinting through life. Stillness slows us down long enough to notice what God has been saying all along.

In stillness, God aligns your heart with His will.
In stillness, He strengthens your inner life for what is coming.
In stillness, He clears the noise so you can hear the next instruction.
In stillness, He rearranges what you cannot reach.
In stillness, He fights battles you cannot fight.

This is why the title says, "When Movement Stops but Miracles Begin." Because there are miracles that begin not when you push, but when you yield. Not when you demand, but when you trust. Not when you rush the process, but when you rest in the God of the process.

The Strength of Holy Silence

Sometimes the most powerful faith statement is not a sermon, but a silence.

It is saying, "God, I will not move until You tell me to." It is the holy restraint that refuses to make permanent decisions from temporary panic. It is the discipline of the spirit that says, "I will not speak out of fear. I will not act out of anxiety. I will wait for God's peace to lead me."

This kind of silence is not emptiness. It is expectancy. It is worship without words. It is faith sitting down in the presence of God and saying, "I trust You even if I do not understand."

And there is a Scripture that anchors this posture with breathtaking clarity:

"The LORD shall fight for you, and ye shall hold your peace."
Exodus 14:14

What a promise. What a command. The Lord will fight. You will hold your peace.

This verse does not pretend there is no battle. It acknowledges the battle, and then it shifts the burden. It takes the weight off your shoulders and places it where it belongs, in the hands of God. It teaches you that peace is not the reward after the fight. Peace is the posture you hold while God fights.

When the Lord fights, you do not have to fight for your identity.
When the Lord fights, you do not have to fight for revenge.
When the Lord fights, you do not have to fight for control.

When the Lord fights, you do not have to fight to be seen. When the Lord fights, you can hold your peace.

Silence is not weakness. Silence is focus. In moments of holy silence, distractions lose their grip and the soul becomes attentive again. There is a sharpened clarity that comes when we stop filling every space with words, explanations, and constant motion. God often works quietly because deep work requires concentration. Loud environments can stir emotion, but they rarely produce lasting formation. The most enduring shaping of the heart often happens away from the crowd, in the hush where God speaks without competing voices.

Holy silence helps the believer hear beyond noise, beyond opinion, beyond urgency and expectation. It creates room for discernment to rise, for wisdom to settle, and for direction to become clear. Silence is not emptiness. It is space, sacred and intentional, where the heart is trained to listen rather than react. In that stillness, the soul learns to pause before rushing, to seek God's mind before chasing human approval, and to wait for what is true rather than what is loud.

And when God Himself seems silent, we must not assume He is distant. God's silence is not disengagement. It is deliberate presence. Sometimes the Lord quiets the outer world so He can address the inner one. Sometimes He withholds immediate answers so trust can deepen and motives can be purified. His quiet is not neglect. It is nearness with purpose, the steady gaze of a Father who is working in ways you cannot yet name, but will one day recognize as faithful.

Faith Reflection

Stillness is the soil where peace grows. It clears the noise long enough for you to hear God again. When everything in you wants to act, pause and pray instead. You might be surprised by what becomes clear when you stop running.

He is not late. He is not ignoring you. He is positioning you.

The still moments of your life are not empty. They are filled with unseen preparation. They are the quiet construction of a future you cannot yet see. They are the hidden strengthening of a heart that will need stability later. They are the gentle pruning of what cannot go with you into your next season.

So, breathe. Release. Let your shoulders drop. Let your jaw unclench. Let your mind stop rehearsing worst case scenarios. Let your heart return to its safest place, the presence of God.

And return again to the Word that steadies anxious souls:

"Be still, and know that I am God."
Psalm 46:10

Knowing God is not only learning facts about Him. It is resting in His character. It is remembering that the One who holds the universe also holds you. It is trusting that even when you do not understand the plan, the Planner is still perfect.

So, if you are standing at a crossroads today, if your heart is tired, if your prayers feel unanswered, and your next step feels uncertain, hear the invitation of this chapter. Be still. Not because the problem is small, but because God is great.

Be still. Not because you do not care, but because you trust. Be still. Not because nothing is happening, but because heaven is working.

Movement may stop, but miracles can begin.

Stillness is a sacred discipline in a world addicted to motion. This chapter teaches that God often asks us to pause—not because nothing is happening, but because He is taking over what we can no longer control. Stillness is trust under restraint.

To be still is to release the illusion that urgency equals faith. It is to choose surrender over striving. God fights battles we cannot win when we stop fighting battles we were never meant to carry.

In stillness, the soul remembers its Anchor. Peace does not come because the storm ends, but because trust deepens. When movement stops, alignment begins—and miracles often follow.

Reflection Guide and Grace Journal

Reflection Guide

1. Where am I striving unnecessarily?

2. What fear surfaces in stillness?

3. How would trust change my response?

Grace Journal Prompt

Lord, teach me holy stillness.

Scripture to Return To

"Be still, and know that I am God." — Psalm 46:10 (KJV)

CHAPTER 7 – WHEN FAITH FEELS FRAGILE

Holding On When You Can Barely Believe

Faith is not always loud. Sometimes it trembles. Sometimes it questions. Sometimes it cries in the dark and whispers, "Lord, I believe, help my unbelief." There are moments when faith does not arrive like a trumpet. It comes like a soft breath, like a bruised prayer that barely makes it past your lips. And yet, even that faint whisper matters to God.

This chapter exists for the believer who feels stretched thin, for the heart that wants to trust but is tired of being strong. It is written for those who have learned that faith is not a straight line, and that spiritual courage sometimes looks like simply staying. Staying in prayer. Staying in hope. Staying in God, even when you do not feel steady. The title, "When Faith Feels Fragile," is not an announcement of defeat. It is an honest confession that there are seasons when the soul feels delicate. But the purpose of this chapter is to show you that fragile faith is still faith, and that God does not abandon you in the trembling. He meets you there.

There are moments when faith feels like glass, beautiful but breakable. When life shatters your plans and leaves you standing barefoot among the pieces, disappointment can make belief feel thin. You try to gather your thoughts, but they scatter. You try to pray, but the words feel heavy. You try to worship, but the song catches in your throat. And you wonder, quietly, if your faith is failing.

But the truth is, your faith may not be failing. It may be revealing. Revealing what you truly depend on. Revealing what you still trust when the comfortable layers are stripped away. Revealing that you are human, and that you need God more than you ever realized.

I have known that kind of fragility. The kind where your prayers sound tired and your hope feels smaller than your pain. The kind where you look at your life and feel as though the "amen" you spoke yesterday has turned into a question today. The kind where you do not want to stop believing, but you do not know how to keep believing with a heart that feels bruised.

Yet even in those fragile moments, God does not step back. He leans closer.

He does not shame your weakness. He strengthens your faith through it. He does not stand over you with disappointment. He kneels beside you with compassion. He does not look at your trembling as a lack of devotion. He sees it as evidence that you are still reaching, still hoping, still choosing Him in the middle of your storm.

Some people have been taught that real faith never wavers, never aches, never questions. But Scripture and life both tell a different story. Faith is not the absence of struggle. Faith is the decision to keep trusting God in the presence of struggle. Faith does not mean you never feel fear. It means fear does not get the final word. Faith does not mean your heart never breaks. It means you bring your broken heart to the One who heals.

God takes the broken pieces of your belief and breathes on them until they glow again. He knows how to restore what feels shattered. He knows how to rebuild what feels unstable. He knows how to take a flicker and fan it into flame. He knows how to take a bruised reed and not break it further. He knows how to take a smoking flax and not snuff it out. The Lord is gentle with fragile things, especially with fragile faith.

And here is a holy surprise. Even a flicker of faith is enough for God to move mountains.

A flicker may feel small to you, but it is not small to Him. Because God's power has never depended on the size of your strength. It depends on the greatness of His own. When you have little, He can still do much. When you feel weak, He can still be strong. When you are down to your last "Lord, help me," heaven is not offended. Heaven responds.

Faith does not mean you never struggle. It means you keep trusting in the middle of the struggle. It means you hold on, not because you feel strong, but because you know God is faithful.

Sometimes holding on looks like reading one verse and letting it carry you for the day. Sometimes holding on looks like praying the same sentence again and again because you do not have the words for a full prayer. Sometimes holding on looks like sitting quietly in God's presence, not performing, not pretending, just being honest. Sometimes holding on looks like tears falling while you whisper, "I am still Yours."

This is so often, we measure faith by how confident we sound. But God measures faith by how deeply we cling. The miracle is not always in how loudly you shout "I believe." The miracle is in how quietly you refuse to let go.

When You Are Barely Holding, God Is Still Holding You

One of the most painful lies fragile faith can believe is the lie that you must be strong for God to love you. But God's love is not earned by your performance. It is revealed in His presence. When faith feels fragile, you are not disqualified. You are being invited into deeper dependence.

The Lord knows how to father the trembling heart. He knows how to shepherd the weary soul. He knows how to stand in the middle of your confusion and still call you His. Your weakness does not scare Him. Your questions do not repel Him. Your tears do not irritate Him. He counts them.

And sometimes, when faith feels fragile, the greatest mercy God gives is not an immediate answer, but a steady peace that keeps you from falling apart while you wait.

"The Lord will fight for you; you need only to be still."
Exodus 14:14
This Scripture speaks directly to the fragile believer who feels pressured to fix everything. It is God saying, "You are not alone in this. The battle is not fully yours. The outcome does not rest on your ability to hold everything together." There are seasons when the strongest act of faith is not movement. It is stillness. It is surrender. It is letting God do what only God can do while you hold your peace.

Stillness does not mean your heart is numb. It means your spirit is anchored. Stillness is not denial. It is trust. It is saying, "Lord, my faith feels fragile, but I will not run from You. I will stay here with You. Fight for me."

When your faith is fragile, you may not have the energy to fight every battle. But you can still choose to rest in God's promise. You can still choose to let Him be your defender. You can still choose to stand, even if you are standing with shaking knees.

Faith Reflection

When faith feels fragile, remember this. God counts tears, not trophies. He never asked you to perform your faith. He asked you to live it, even in the cracks. He asked you to keep coming. To keep leaning. To keep returning to Him, even when your emotions are uncertain.

Faith is less about certainty and more about surrender. It is trusting God when you do not see the outcome because you have already seen His character. You have seen His faithfulness in other seasons. You have seen Him carry you when you did not know how you would survive. You have seen Him open doors that once seemed sealed. You have seen Him comfort you in losses that could have destroyed you. You have seen enough of who He is to trust Him again, even now.

So if your hands are trembling, lift them anyway. If your hope is small, speak it anyway. If your heart feels bruised, bring it anyway. Faith that feels fragile is still faith, and God honors it.

Your fragile faith may not look impressive to people, but it is precious to God. Because it is real. It is humble. It is honest. It says, "Lord, I cannot do this alone." And that confession is the doorway to grace.

There is a kind of strength that grows only when you admit you are weak. There is a kind of peace that comes only when you stop pretending you are fine. There is a kind of healing that begins when you bring God the truth of where you are, not the image of where you want to appear.

So let this chapter be your gentle reminder. You are not failing because you are fragile. You are human. And you are held.

Held by a God who does not break bruised things.
Held by a Savior who understands suffering.
Held by a Spirit who intercedes when your words run out.
Held by the One who remains faithful even when your faith feels thin.
And if all you can do today is whisper, then whisper.
Heaven hears whispers.

"The Lord will fight for you; you need only to be still."
Exodus 14:14
Let that Word steady you. Let it rest on your chest like a warm blanket on a cold night. Let it silence the fear that says it is all up to you. It is not all up to you. God is with you. God is for you. God is fighting for you. And even fragile faith can hold on long enough for God to show His strength.

Be still. Breathe. You are not alone.

Faith does not always feel strong. Sometimes it trembles, whispers, or simply refuses to let go. This chapter honors fragile faith, the kind that survives not by confidence, but by honesty and dependence.

God does not shame weak faith. He strengthens it. Fragility does not disqualify you; it draws God closer. Even whispered prayers are heard. Even trembling trust is precious. Faith that feels fragile is still faith. It clings not because it is powerful, but because God is faithful. In weakness, God proves His gentleness and His strength.

Reflection Guide and Grace Journal

Reflection Guide

1. When has my faith felt fragile?

2. What lie tells me weakness disqualifies me?

3. How has God met me gently?

Grace Journal Prompt

Lord, meet me in my weakness.

Scripture to Return To

"The LORD shall fight for you, and ye shall hold your peace." — Exodus 14:14 (KJV)

Chapter 8 – THE OIL OF ENDURANCE

Grace to Keep Going When Strength Runs Out

Endurance is not the absence of pain. It is the presence of purpose in the middle of it.

There is a kind of strength that looks impressive in public but disappears in private. It can perform, it can smile, it can keep up appearances, but it cannot survive the long night. Endurance is different. Endurance is not a burst of energy. It is a holy staying power. It is the steady decision to keep walking when the road gets rough, to keep praying when the answers feel delayed, to keep believing when the outcome is unclear, and to keep trusting God even when your own strength has run out.

This chapter is written for those moments.

It is written for the believer who has done everything they know to do and still feels weary. It is written for the servant of God who has carried others, lifted burdens, spoken encouragement, and now feels like their own soul is tired. It is written for the heart that has said "yes" repeatedly and now finds itself in a season where the "yes" costs more than it used to. It is written to explain the essence, meaning, and purpose of this title, "The Oil of Endurance," and to remind you that God does not waste your pressing. He does not waste your tears. He does not waste your delay. He uses it all to produce something precious.

Because oil is never produced without pressure.

The Pressing That Produces Oil

There are seasons when your anointing must pass through the crushing, because oil does not appear in a gentle season. The olive does not release its oil until it is pressed. Likewise, you do not always know the depth of your strength until life squeezes you. Pressure reveals what is inside you. It exposes what is genuine. It separates surface faith from rooted faith. It shows you where you have been leaning on comfort, applause, or control, and it invites you to lean instead on God.

What feels like breaking is often God's refining, turning your trials into testimony, and your pain into purpose.

There is a sacred mystery in the pressing. It is not comfortable, but it is fruitful. It is not easy, but it is meaningful. The crushing does not mean God is angry with you. It often means God is developing you. Some things cannot be formed in ease. Some kinds of character cannot be taught comfortably. Some forms of spiritual authority only come through endurance, through staying, through continuing when everything in you wants to quit.

Sometimes God is pressing out the oil that will sustain you in the next season. Sometimes He is pressing out the oil that will heal someone else through your story. Sometimes He is pressing out an anointing that cannot be stolen because it was forged in fire, matured in waiting, and strengthened in pain.

When Strength Runs Out, Grace Steps In

There were moments when I thought I could not take another step. Moments when my mind felt heavy, my heart felt bruised, and my prayers sounded tired. I reached the edge of what I thought I could carry. And that is where I discovered something holy.

Grace came like oxygen, invisible yet essential.

It whispered, "You can endure this because I am in you."

Grace does not always remove the weight, but it strengthens you under it. Grace does not always erase the challenge, but it enables you to survive it. Grace does not always change the environment, but it changes you in the environment. Grace is God's steady presence supplying what your human strength cannot produce.

And that grace does not arrive as condemnation. It does not say, "Why are you tired?" It says, "Come closer." It does not shame your exhaustion. It covers it. It does not demand a performance. It offers a hand. It meets you in your weakness and becomes your strength.

Every tear watered a new level of endurance. Every disappointment taught me resilience. And every delay was not a denial, but divine training.

Delay is painful because it tests more than patience. It tests trust. It tests whether you believe God is good even when He is slow. It tests whether you will keep worshiping when you do not get what you want quickly. It tests whether you will keep showing up, not only when the sky is clear, but when the clouds linger.

But delay can also be a teacher.

It teaches you how to love God for who He is, not only for what He gives. It teaches you how to stand without leaning on quick answers. It teaches you how to keep moving with a quiet confidence that God is working even when you cannot see it.

The Costly Gift of Endurance

The oil of endurance is costly. It requires faith that refuses to quit. It demands trust when the outcome is unclear. It asks you to keep obeying while your feelings argue with your obedience. It calls you to keep praying when prayers feel unanswered. It calls you to keep doing good when doing good feels unnoticed.

Endurance does not always feel heroic. Sometimes endurance looks like simply getting out of bed. Sometimes it looks like doing the next right thing with tears in your eyes. Sometimes it looks like worshiping without emotion, purely by choice. Sometimes it looks like staying faithful in secret, where no one claps, no one sees, and no one understands.

But endurance produces something priceless.

It produces character that cannot be shaken and faith that cannot be stolen.

A faith forged in ease can be easily shaken. But a faith forged in fire becomes steady. A faith built on comfort can collapse when the storm comes. But a faith built through endurance learns how to stand. The kind of believer who endures becomes a living testimony. Not because life was easy, but because God was faithful. Not because pain was absent, but because grace was present.

Stillness in the Middle of the Fight

One of the strangest truths about endurance is that sometimes it requires movement, and sometimes it requires stillness. Sometimes endurance means keep walking. Sometimes endurance means stop striving.

There are seasons when God does not ask you to fight your way into promise. He asks you to hold your peace and let Him fight for you.

"The Lord will fight for you; you need only to be still."
Exodus 14:14

This Scripture is not for people who have no battles. It is for people surrounded by them. It is for moments when the heart wants to panic, the mind wants to race, and the hands want to force. The Lord says, "Be still." Not because nothing is happening, but because heaven is working. Stillness is not emptiness. Stillness is trust.

And there is another word that grounds the weary soul when the process feels long:

"Be still, and know that I am God."
Psalm 46:10
Knowing God is not only understanding His plans. It is resting in His character. It is remembering that He is sovereign when you feel uncertain. It is believing that God has not lost control because you feel weak. It is trusting that His timing is wise, His love is steady, and His presence is real.

Stillness becomes a form of endurance. It becomes the spiritual discipline of refusing to let anxiety lead you. It becomes the quiet strength of letting God be God, while you breathe and obey.

Faith Reflection

Endurance is not glamorous, but it is glorious.

It is the quiet strength that says, "I am not finished yet." When others see exhaustion, God sees evolution. When others see delay, God sees development. When others see weakness, God sees a vessel being strengthened for greater use.

Do not despise your process. It is pressing out the oil that will heal others. Your endurance will not only sustain you. It will bless someone else. One day, your story will become a lamp for someone else's dark valley. The oil in your life will become comfort for someone else's pain. The testimony you are living now will become the encouragement someone else needs to keep going.

Every time you rise again, heaven celebrates your obedience. Every time you choose to pray again, to trust again, to worship again, to love again, to forgive again, to show up again, heaven honors that quiet faith.

So, keep walking. Keep believing. Keep becoming.

Not because you are trying to prove something, but because God is producing something. Your oil is proof that you survived the crushing and that you carry something worth pouring.

Even if your strength feels low, grace is not low. Even if your heart feels tired, God is not tired. Even if your faith feels strained, God is still faithful.

Hold your peace. Do the next right thing. Take the next step. And when you cannot take another step, be still and let the Lord fight for you.

"The Lord will fight for you; you need only to be still."
Exodus 14:14

Endurance is not dramatic; it is faithful. It is the decision to keep going when strength fades and answers delay. God uses pressure to produce oil—something lasting, healing, and valuable. Grace meets you where strength ends. Endurance formed through pain carries authority that comfort never could. God uses your perseverance to bless not only you, but others who will draw strength from your testimony. What feels like crushing is often preparation. God is producing something in you that cannot be formed any other way.

Reflection Guide and Grace Journal

Reflection Guide

1. What season of endurance am I in?

2. How has pressure revealed growth?

3. What would trusting God's process change?

Grace Journal Prompt

Lord, show me what You are producing.

Scripture to Return To:

"Be still and know that I am God." — Psalm 46:10 (KJV)

CHAPTER 9 – THE COURAGE TO BEGIN AGAIN

When Grace Gives You a Second Sunrise

Starting over is not a sign of failure. It is evidence of faith.

There are people who assume that beginning again means you lost your way, that restarting is proof you were not strong enough, not spiritual enough, not wise enough. But that is not heaven's language. Heaven calls beginning again mercy. Heaven calls it restoration. Heaven calls it the quiet power of grace touching what life tried to ruin and saying, "This is not the end."

Life will break. Dreams will pause. People will walk away. Plans will unravel in ways you never rehearsed. Sometimes the very thing you thought would last becomes the thing that collapses. Sometimes what you poured yourself into changes, disappears, or dies. And when that happens, something inside you wants to withdraw, to harden, to stop hoping. Yet the Spirit of God keeps whispering the same invitation, not as a slogan, but as a lifeline.

Begin again.

This chapter is written for the soul standing at the edge of a new start, looking at the road ahead with mixed emotions. Part of you wants to move forward. Another part of you is afraid to hope again. This chapter exists to explain the essence, meaning, and purpose of its title, "The Courage to Begin Again," and to remind you that new beginnings are not reserved for perfect people. New beginnings are for the weary, the humbled, the wounded, the repentant, the unsure, and the faithful. New beginnings are what God does.

The Mountain Inside You

Sometimes the hardest mountain to climb is not the one before you, but the one inside you.

The mountain inside you is the fear of trying after falling. It is the trembling question that asks, "What if I fail again?" It is the memory of what broke last time. It is the shame that tries to keep you chained to yesterday. It is the ache of disappointment that makes your hands reluctant to build again. It is the quiet voice that says, "Do not risk it. Do not trust it. Do not start."

But beloved, God specializes in new beginnings.

He does not consult your past to design your future. He is not limited by your missteps, your losses, your regrets, or the opinions that others formed about you. God sees more than what you did. He sees who you are becoming. He sees the work He is doing inside you. He sees your heart when it is bruised but still reaching. He sees your tears and calls them seeds. He sees the places you thought disqualified you, and He turns them into testimony.

He rebuilds you, not because you are strong, but because His mercy is endless.

This is what grace does. Grace does not deny what happened. Grace does not pretend the ashes are not real. Grace simply refuses to let ashes be the final chapter. Grace steps into the ruins and speaks resurrection. Grace gives you a second sunrise.

Ashes and the Voice of God

I have stood before seasons that looked like ashes, and still, God spoke life.

There are times when you look at your life and feel as though everything you trusted has been reduced to smoke. The future you pictured is gone. The stability you depended on feels shaken. The dream you loved seems buried. And in that space, it is easy to confuse brokenness with abandonment. It is easy to believe that if things fell apart, God must have left.

But God reminded me of something sacred. Resurrection is not a one-time event. It is a rhythm of grace.

It is the quiet pattern of God bringing life out of dead places, hope out of heartbreak, strength out of weakness, and purpose out of pain. It is God repeatedly proving that endings do not intimidate Him. He is the God who stands at graves and still speaks. He is the God who walks into locked rooms and still brings peace. He is the God who turns losses into lessons, tears into oil, and waiting into wisdom.

Every sunrise declares, "Yesterday ended, but My mercy did not."

That is the heartbeat of this chapter. Every sunrise is a sermon. It preaches without words. It says the night did not win. It says the darkness could not hold forever. It says God still rules over time and seasons. It says there is still breath in your lungs, still grace in your story, still purpose in your steps.

You will never be too broken to be used.
You will never be too late for redemption.
And you will never be too lost for God to find you again.

These are not sentimental lines. They are spiritual realities. The enemy wants you to believe that your failure is final. God declares that your failure can become fertile ground for humility, wisdom, and transformation. The enemy wants you to believe your delay is disqualification. God says delay can be development. The enemy wants you to believe you are too far gone. God says His arm is not too short to save, restore, and rebuild.

What Courage Really Means

The courage to begin again is not about confidence. It is about conviction.

It is not the absence of fear. It is obedience in the presence of fear. It is saying, "Lord, I trust You more than I fear what is next." It is moving forward with shaking knees but steady faith. It is taking a step without seeing the whole staircase. It is building again even if you still feel tender. It is opening your heart again, not because you are careless, but because you believe God is faithful.

Beginning again does not mean you pretend you were not hurt. It means you refuse to let hurt become your master. It means you allow God to heal you without freezing you. It means you let wisdom grow where wounds once lived. It means you let the Lord strengthen your boundaries and soften your heart at the same time.

Sometimes, beginning again is not loud. It is quiet. It looks like making one phone call. It looks like writing one page. It looks like praying for one honest prayer. It looks like getting up after you fell and choosing not to lie down in despair. It looks like you are forgiving yourself. It looks like letting God redeem the part of your story you have been ashamed to revisit.

Faith Reflection

The same God who started your story has not stopped writing.

Your detours are not denials. They are divine redirections. Sometimes God lets what you built fall apart so He can rebuild it stronger, purer, and more aligned with His will. This is painful, because we get attached to what we build. We get attached to the version of life we imagined. But God loves you too much to leave you trapped in a structure that cannot hold your destiny.

Sometimes He allows collapse because collapse exposes what was never stable. Sometimes He allows loss because loss reveals what you have been leaning on instead of Him. Sometimes He allows endings because endings are the doorway into beginnings that could not happen any other way.

You do not need to understand the process to walk in obedience. You just need to take the first step, again.

That is where many believers get stuck. They want clarity before obedience. They want guarantees before surrender. They want to understand everything before moving forward. But faith does not require full explanation. Faith requires trust. Faith requires the willingness to take the step God is asking for today, not the step you wish He would explain for tomorrow.

The road may look unfamiliar, but grace knows the way.

Grace is the hand of God guiding you when you do not feel ready. Grace is the favor of God opening what you cannot force. Grace is the mercy of God lifting you when you feel weak. Grace is the presence of God walking beside you when the path feels lonely.

And the same God who met you in your valley will greet you at your next beginning.

Stillness Before the Next Step

Before some new beginnings, God calls you into stillness, not to delay you, but to anchor you.

Because some people begin again out of panic. They move too quickly to escape the pain of what ended. They rush into new chapters without letting God heal the old one. But God is kind. He does not just push you forward. He steadies you.

"The Lord will fight for you; you need only to be still."
Exodus 14:14
This Scripture is a shelter for restarting the heart. It reminds you that you do not have to fight your way into your future. You do not have to defend your redemption to people who

only knew your past. You do not have to force doors open with anxious hands. The Lord will fight for you. He will defend what He ordained. He will protect what He promised. He will guide you into what is next.

Sometimes your first step is not action. Sometimes your first step is stillness. Stillness is the place where fear calms down enough for faith to speak. Stillness is where you release the need to control and receive the strength to obey. Stillness is where you let God remind you that your future is not built by panic, but by promise.

So, breathe. Let your shoulders relax. Let your heart unclench. Let grace steady you. The God who calls you is also the God who covers you.

Begin again. Not because you are fearless, but because God is faithful. Begin again. Not because you have all the answers, but because you know the One who does. Begin again. Not because your past was perfect, but because your Redeemer is.

And when the second sunrise comes, and it will come, you will look back and realize that God was not punishing you by allowing what ended. He was preparing you for what had to begin.

Beginning again calls for humility that bows low, trust that reaches forward, and courage that stands up even while the heart still trembles. This chapter gently reminds us that God is not intimidated by endings. Endings do not alarm Him or limit Him. He is the God who restores, the One who gathers what feels scattered and rebuilds what feels beyond repair.

New beginnings are not evidence of failure. They are acts of faith. They are the quiet decision to believe that God is still writing, even when a page has closed.

Grace does not erase the past. It redeems it. God does not rebuild with haste, as though He is in a rush to prove something. He rebuilds with wisdom, with tenderness, and with purpose. Beginning again often starts in small places, with simple obedience rather than loud confidence. Sometimes the bravest step is not the one that feels fearless, but the one that is taken while still afraid.

God does not consult your failures when designing your future. He does not measure your tomorrow by your yesterday. He invites you forward, not because you are unshakable, but because He is faithful. And when you cannot see the whole road ahead, He asks you to walk with Him one step at a time, letting His faithfulness become the ground beneath your feet.

Reflection Guide and Grace Journal

Reflection Guide

1. What ending am I grieving right now
2. What fear is resisting my willingness to begin again
3. What step of obedience is set before me today

Grace Journal Prompt

Lord, give me courage to begin again.

Scripture to Return To

"The LORD shall fight for you, and ye shall hold your peace."
Exodus 14:14 (KJV)

CHAPTER 10 – THE UNSTOPPABLE HOPE

The Light That Refuses to Die Out

Hope is not fragile. Hope is eternal.

It may bend beneath the weight of sorrow, but it never breaks. It may grow silent in the dark, but it never stops breathing. True hope is not based on what we see, but on what we know, that God is still good, even when life is not. That is the first truth this chapter must speak into your soul. There are seasons when your surroundings look like evidence against God's goodness. There are moments when the heart feels bruised by loss, when prayers feel delayed, when the future looks like a hallway with no lights. Yet even there, hope does not die. It may whisper instead of shout, but it remains.

This chapter exists because many people believe hope is an emotion. They think hope is only what you feel when life is going well, when the diagnosis is favorable, when the bills are paid, when relationships are stable, when the plan is working. But "The Unstoppable Hope" is something deeper. It is not shallow optimism. It is not pretending pain is not real. It is not ignoring grief. It is a spiritual force that rises from God's breath within you. It is the light that refuses to die out because it is lit by the Lord Himself.

That is the essence and purpose of this title. "The Unstoppable Hope" is not a compliment to human willpower. It is a testimony to divine presence. It is heaven's insistence in the human heart that says, "This is not the end." It is the inner strength that rises when everything around you has fallen apart. It is the quiet courage that still shows up, still believes, still prays, still dreams, even when you do not have clear reasons to feel confident.

Hope is the whisper that says, "This is not the end."

And sometimes that whisper is the only sound strong enough to hold you.

Hope That Breathes in the Dark

I have walked through nights that felt endless. Nights where the mind would not rest. Nights where grief sat on the chest like a stone. Nights where I searched heaven for a sign and found only silence. But even in those nights, something in me refused to quit. Something kept saying, "Keep going." Something kept reaching for God even when my hands were trembling.

Every dawn reminded me that no darkness can cancel God's promise.

The sun does not ask the night for permission to rise. It does not negotiate with the shadows. Morning simply arrives. In the same way, hope keeps arriving in the lives of God's people. It rises because God is faithful. It rises because mercy is new. It rises because the Lord does not abandon His own. You may not be able to explain your endurance, but that endurance is often proof of hope working inside you.

And let us be honest. Hope is not always pretty. Sometimes hope is messy. Sometimes hope is holding on while crying. Sometimes hope continues even when you feel exhausted. Sometimes hope is sitting in the waiting room with a prayer you have repeated so many times you wonder if it still has power, but you pray it again anyway. Hope is not always a song. Sometimes hope is a sigh. Sometimes hope is a simple decision to make it through the next hour with God.

But even then, hope remains.

Hope Is Not Denial. Hope Is Defiance.

Hope is not denial. Hope is defiance.

It stares at the storm and declares, "You cannot take what God has ordained." It looks at the wind, the waves, the loss, the delay, the betrayal, the disappointment, and it refuses to accept that pain is the final voice. Hope refuses to let darkness write the ending of your story. Hope refuses to let fear become your prophet. Hope refuses to allow grief to steal your future.

This is why hope is unstoppable. Because true hope is not rooted in circumstances. True hope is rooted in God.

There is something divine in the human spirit that refuses to quit. That is the breath of God inside you. That is the reason you are still here. That is the reason you still believe, still dream, still show up. You may have been wounded, but you are still reaching. You may have been disappointed, but you are still praying. You may have lost much, but you have not lost everything, because you have not lost God.

Hope is heaven's fingerprint on your heart.

It is the mark of divine love that refuses to let you go. It is the imprint of God's promise inside your inner life. It is not something you manufacture by human strength. It is something God plants by His Spirit.

Even when your plans collapse, hope rebuilds. Even when your faith shakes, hope steadies your soul. And even when your tears fall, hope plants seeds in them, seeds that grow into testimony.

Some tears are not simply expressions of pain. Some tears are water for the future. God knows how to take what hurt you and turn it into what heals others. He knows how to use your survival as someone else's sign that they can survive too. He knows how to turn your story into a lamp. He knows how to make your scars speak.

The Light That Refuses to Die Out

The title says, "The Light That Refuses to Die Out," because hope has a stubborn glow. It may dim, but it does not disappear. It may flicker, but it does not go out. Why? Because hope does not live on your strength alone. Hope is fueled by the faithfulness of God.

When you feel like you have nothing left, hope reminds you that God is still present. When you feel like your prayers are small, hope reminds you that God hears whispers. When you feel like your future is uncertain, hope reminds you that God is already in your tomorrow. When you feel like your heart is breaking, hope reminds you that the Lord is close to the brokenhearted and that He heals.

Hope is not a fragile candle placed in a windy place and expected to survive on its own. Hope is the fire of God lit within you, and no storm can extinguish what God sustains.

Faith Reflection

Hope is not an emotion. Hope is a weapon.

Use it when you are weary. Wield it when you are wounded. Let it remind you that even if today ends in tears, tomorrow still holds resurrection.

That is not a promise that tomorrow will be painless. It is a promise that tomorrow is not godless. It is a promise that the Lord who carried you today will still be present tomorrow. It is a promise that suffering does not have the final word. It is a promise that joy is not dead, even if it feels distant. It is a promise that God can lift what feels buried.

Hope outlasts pain.
Hope outshines fear.
Hope outlives death.

You are here today not because everything was easy, but because hope, unstoppable, unshakable, unbreakable, refused to let you go.

So, lift your head, beloved.

There is glory after grief, laughter after loss, and purpose after pain. Not because life becomes perfect, but because God remains faithful. Not because you never struggle again, but because God strengthens you again and again. Hope is not finished with you yet.

And when your heart feels tired, when fear starts to speak too loudly, when the world's weight presses down, return to the Scriptures that steady the soul in the storm.

"The Lord will fight for you; you need only to be still." Exodus 14:14

This verse is not a decoration for calm days. It is a lifeline for hard days. It reminds you that you are not alone in the battle. It reminds you that God takes ownership of what concerns you. It reminds you that you do not have to fight your way into peace. Sometimes you hold your peace while God fights.

And when your spirit is restless, when questions churn inside you, when you feel tempted to run ahead of God, return again to this holy command.

"Be still and know that I am God."
Psalm 46:10

Knowing God is not merely understanding His plan. It is trusting His character. It is resting in His sovereignty. It is letting His greatness calm your panic. It is remembering that He is God over storms, over delays, over losses, and over nation. Hope is not mere optimism, a bright thought trying to outrun reality. Hope is holy defiance rooted in God. It refuses to let pain have the final word. It endures, not because life is gentle, but because God is faithful. Even in the thickest darkness, hope still breathes, like a small flame sheltered in the hands of the Almighty.

Unstoppable hope is not born from ease. It is forged in endurance. It stays because God stays. Hope is heaven's imprint on the human heart, a sacred light no storm can snuff out, no season can bury, no sorrow can silence for long.

And you are here for a reason. You are still standing, still praying, still reaching, because hope did not let go of you. That hope is not finished with you yet. God is still at work, still restoring, still unfolding what you cannot yet see.

Reflection Guide & Grace Journal

Reflection Guide

1. Where has hope survived in me, even while pain pressed hard
2. What voices or thoughts try to convince me that my story is over
3. In what ways does trusting God breathe fresh life into my hope

Grace Journal Prompt

Lord, let hope rise again in me.

Scripture to Return To:

"Be still and know that I am God."
Psalm 46:10 (KJV)

ns, over generations, over your life.

Reflection Guide and Grace Journal

Reflection on the Chapter

1. What challenge taught you the true meaning of courage?
2. How did your faith carry you when everything else failed?
3. What promise from God are you holding onto today?

Grace Journal – Any thoughts?

"Be still, and know that I am God."
Psalm 46:10

Closing Reflection

This is not just the end of a book. It is the beginning of your reawakening.

Carry this truth wherever you go. Carry it into your home, your workplace, your waiting room, your healing season, your rebuilding season, your prayer closet, your next beginning.

You are proof that hope still works. You are the living evidence that faith still heals.

And if you can breathe, you can hope again. If you can whisper, you can pray again. If you can take one step, you can rise again. The light has not gone out. The Lord is still with you. Hope is still alive.

CONCLUSION

When the Storm Doesn't Get the Last Word

If you have made it to these closing pages, it is not because life was gentle. It is because grace kept meeting you in the middle of what was heavy. This volume began with a simple but holy insistence: hope is not a fragile wish we whisper into the dark—it is a divine strategy placed by heaven inside human hearts. And now, at the end of Volume I, that insistence becomes an invitation: do not treat what you've read as information—receive it as formation. The deepest work of this book is not in finishing chapters, but in becoming the kind of person who can keep believing when the evidence is delayed, the answers are quiet, and the process is long.

1) Hope is not an emotion—It is an anchor

One of the most dangerous misunderstandings we carry is that hope is what we feel when life is cooperating. But this manuscript teaches the opposite: real hope is what remains when life is not cooperating—when the ground is shaking and you need a foundation that cannot crack. The Living Rock is not a metaphor meant for calm days. It is survival truth for the days when your hands are tired, your mind is loud, and your heart is trying to remember how to sing again.

So, the question this book leaves you with is not simply, "Do I have hope?" but "Where is my hope anchored?" When your hope is anchored in outcomes, it rises and falls with circumstances. When your hope is anchored in God's character, it becomes unkillable—because God does not shift when seasons do.

2) Stillness is not passivity—It is spiritual intelligence

Perhaps the most repeated instruction across these pages is also one of the most difficult for anxious hearts: be still. The book does not treat stillness as silence without purpose; it presents stillness as trust with roots—refusing to panic while God performs what only He can do. "The LORD shall fight for you, and ye shall hold your peace" is not a decorative verse in this manuscript. It is a posture. It is the shifting of weight—from your shoulders to God's hands. And "Be still and know that I am God" is not a suggestion for calmer personalities—it is a divine command for seasons when you are tempted to strive, force, and rush the process.

Here is the thought that may change how you live after you close this book: some miracles begin not when you push harder, but when you yield deeper. Stillness is not the absence of movement; it is the presence of alignment.

3) Divine protection does not cancel warfare—It limits it

This volume's special section makes something plain: God's protection does not mean you will have no battles; it means you are not unguarded in them. The manuscript frames calling as covenant—not self-importance, but God's responsibility toward what He appoints. That is why it repeatedly returns to this stabilizing truth: when God calls, He covers; when God appoints, He defends; when God speaks, His Word stands.

So, if you have felt contested, questioned, opposed, or stretched, let this be your recalibration: opposition is not proof you are outside God's will; sometimes it is proof you are standing near purpose.

4) Authority is not noise—It is alignment

In a world that celebrates visibility, this manuscript honors a different kind of strength: the strength formed in hidden obedience. It insists that true authority is not arrogance, volume, or self-promotion, but spiritual weight that comes from alignment—proven by endurance and refined by faithfulness.

This is an uncomfortable but liberating idea: you do not need constant applause to be faithful. A life can carry authority without a microphone because heaven measures authority by fruit, not by noise. And that means your quiet endurance—your continued "yes" in unseen places—may be one of the strongest evidences that God is shaping you for longevity.

5) Delay is not denial—It can be protection

This book repeatedly reframes waiting, not as wasted time, but as development. The waiting room is God's workshop, where He is not only preparing what He promised, but preparing you to carry what He promised. God uses time as a tool for aligning resources, readiness, and character because some blessings are too heavy for an unprepared spirit.

So, when the door seems shut, the timeline unclear, and the season silent, the question becomes: what if the delay you resent is the protection you will one day thank God for? Waiting, in this volume, is not spiritual weakness. Waiting is spiritual maturity—learning to trust God's wisdom when your emotions demand speed.

6) Pain can become purpose when it is interpreted in God

This manuscript does not glorify pain—but it refuses to waste it. It teaches that purpose is not only a promise; it is a process, and sometimes that process hurts. Yet the pain is reinterpreted: not always punishment, but preparation; not always rejection, but refining; not always burial, but planting.

If you have been pressed, you are not automatically being destroyed. You may be developing.

7) Fragile faith is still faith—and God is gentle with it

One of the most tender contributions of this volume is its refusal to shame the trembling believer. It declares that faith is not always loud—sometimes it whispers, sometimes it cries, sometimes it says, "Lord, I believe, help my unbelief." And yet it insists: fragile faith is still faith, and God meets you in the trembling with compassion, not condemnation.

So, if your faith felt thin while reading, let the truth remain thick: God counts tears, not trophies. And if all you can offer is a whisper, remember—heaven hears whispers.

8) Beginning again is not failure; it is grace in motion

This volume restores dignity to the restart. It calls beginning again mercy, restoration, and the quiet power of grace touching ruins and saying, "This is not the end." It teaches that courage is not the absence of fear; it is obedience in the presence of fear—taking a step without seeing the whole staircase.

So, if you are standing at the edge of a new start, hear the book's steady voice: begin again—not because you are fearless, but because God is faithful.

9) The final message: hope is unstoppable because God is alive

The book's final movement insists that hope is not denial; hope is defiance, and it refuses to let fear become your prophet or pain become your final voice. Hope is the light that refuses to die out—not because you are endlessly strong, but because God sustains what He ignites.

A Closing Charge

Do not let this book remain on a shelf as a memory. Let it become a mirror—and a map.

- When your life shakes, return to the Rock.
- When fear grows loud, keep trusting in the shadows.
- When disappointment repeats, whisper again: "I still believe."
- When you are pressed, remember: oil is produced through pressure—and grace meets you there.
- When waiting stretches, refuse to call it wasted—heaven is working.
- When your faith trembles, do not run—stay, and let God hold you.
- When a chapter ends, do not assume your story ended—begin again.
- And when the storm speaks loudly, remember: God's promise speaks longer.

Final Reflection Question

Before you turn the last page, hold this question in your spirit long enough for it to answer you: What would change in your life if you truly believed that hope is not finished with you yet?

May your next season be marked not by the absence of storms, but by the presence of unshakable peace. May your waiting produce wisdom. May your pain produce oil. May your stillness produce clarity. And may the hope God placed within you rise again—quietly, steadily, and unstoppable.

About the Author

Prophetess Dr. Marie Scott Wilson is a global prophetic author, mentor, humanitarian, and a voice for the voiceless. Her life and work are devoted to restoring hope, strengthening faith, and defending human dignity in places where it has been diminished or denied. With a rare blend of spiritual depth, wisdom, and quiet authority, she writes to meet readers in real-life moments, especially in seasons of uncertainty. Her words guide the weary toward endurance, bring clarity to the confused, and offer renewal to those who feel depleted.

As Founder and Chief Executive Officer of multiple faith-based humanitarian and advocacy initiatives within the Marie Global ecosystem, Dr. Scott Wilson provides visionary leadership across spiritual formation, human rights advocacy, anti-human trafficking work, youth and women's empowerment, governance mentoring, and community development in diverse global contexts. She is recognized for building systems of care that uplift the overlooked and for creating pathways of support for individuals and communities pushed to the margins. Her commitment to justice and compassion is not confined to ideas or statements. It is demonstrated through service, advocacy, and consistent action on behalf of people whose stories are often ignored.

Dr. Scott Wilson's personal life is marked by devotion, strength, and nurture. As a devoted wife and spiritual mother to many, both biological and non-biological, she is known for cultivating lives marked by steady care, wisdom, and love. Those who encounter her ministry often speak of her ability to carry truth without harshness and to offer correction without breaking a bruised spirit. Her understanding of endurance, waiting, and renewal has been shaped by decades of lived experience, resilience in the face of adversity, and unwavering trust in God's faithfulness.

Her book, *The Unstoppable Hopefulness*, is not written from a distance, but from testimony. Dr. Scott Wilson writes as one who has walked through pressing seasons, carried prayers that seemed unanswered, and learned how to remain steady while trusting God's timing. Her devotional voice is both intimate and prophetic. It offers readers more than encouragement because it also provides spiritual formation that strengthens the inner life. She calls believers to anchor their hope in the character of God, to discern purpose even in pain, and to begin again with courage when life demands it.

Dr. Scott Wilson writes from Johnston, Iowa, in the United States, with a heart committed to healing and justice. Her message reaches beyond borders, reminding the weary that God's silence is not His absence and that, even in hidden seasons, He is still at work. Through her ministry, advocacy, and writing, she continues to lift the fallen, strengthen the faith of the struggling, and speak dignity over lives treated as disposable. Her life stands as a living witness that hope can endure, faith can rise again, and God remains faithful through every season.

References

- Holy Bible, King James Version. (1769/2017). Cambridge University Press.
- Lewis, C. S. (1952). *Mere Christianity.* HarperCollins.
- Meyer, J. (2008). *Battlefield of the Mind: Winning the Battle in Your Mind.* FaithWords.
- Jakes, T. D. (2010). *Reposition Yourself: Living Life Without Limits.* Atria Books
- Wilson, M. S. H. (2025). *The Unstoppable Hopefulness — A Prophetic Journey of Faith, Resilience & Hope.* MARIE Global Publishing.
- MARIE Global Faith & Peace Editorial Board. (2025). *MARIE Global Governance Faith and Peace Cycle Policy Guideline Edition 2025–2030.* MARIE

www.ingramcontent.com/pod-product-compliance
Lightning Source LLC
Chambersburg PA
CBHW030221170426
43194CB00007BA/824